PROFESSIONAL STUDIO TECHN
DESIGN ESSENTIALS

Luanne Seymour Cohen ▪ Russell Brown ▪ Lisa Jeans ▪ Tanya Wendling

Adobe Press
Mountain View, California

Patents Pending.

Library of Congress Catalog No.: 92-072409

ISBN: 0-672-48538-9

2 3 4 5 6 7 8 9 10

The information in this book is furnished for informational use only, is subject to change without notice, and should not be construed as a commitment by Adobe Systems Incorporated. Adobe Systems Incorporated assumes no responsibility for any errors or inaccuracies that may appear in this book. The software described in this book is furnished under license and may only be used or copied in accordance with the terms of such license.

PostScript™ is a trademark of Adobe Systems Incorporated ("Adobe"), registered in the United States and elsewhere. PostScript can refer both to the PostScript language as specified by Adobe and to Adobe's implementation of its PostScript language interpreter.

Any references to "PostScript printers," "PostScript files," or "PostScript drivers" refer, respectively, to printers, files and driver programs written in or supporting the PostScript language. References in this book to the "PostScript language" are intended to emphasize Adobe's standard definition of that language.

Adobe, the Adobe Press logo, Adobe Caslon, Adobe Collector's Edition, Adobe Illustrator, Adobe Photoshop, Adobe Separator, Adobe Streamline, Adobe Type Manager, Adobe Wood Type, Birch, Lithos, Minion, PostScript, and Willow are trademarks of Adobe Systems Incorporated, which may be registered in certain jurisdictions. Berthold City is a registered trademark and Walbaum is a trademark of H. Berthold AG. Helvetica, Industria and Künstler Script are trademarks of Linotype-Hell AG and/or its subsidiaries. ITC Stone is a registered trademark of International Typeface Corporation. Futura is a registered trademark of Fundicion Tipografica Neufville S.A. Ryumin is a trademark of Morisawa and Company Limited. Gill Sans is a trademark of The Monotype Corporation plc. which is registered in the US Pat & TM Off. and elsewhere. Reporter is a trademark of J. Wagner. Eurostile is a trademark of Nebiolo. Revue is a trademark of Esselte Pendaflex Corporation in the U.S.A., of Letraset Ltd. Canada in Canada, and of Esselte Letraset elsewhere. Macintosh is a registered trademark of Apple Computer, Inc. PageMaker is a registered trademark of Aldus Corporation. All other brand or product names are trademarks or registered trademarks of their respective holders.

*Pantone, Inc.'s check-standard trademark for color reproduction and color reproduction materials.

Printed in the United States of America.

Published simultaneously in Canada.

Published and distributed to the trade by Hayden, a division of Prentice Hall Computer Publishing. For information, address Hayden, 11711 N. College Avenue, Carmel, IN 46032   1-800-428-5331.

DESIGN ESSENTIALS

Credits

Editor: Tanya Wendling

Book Design/Illustration: Lisa Jeans, Luanne S. Cohen

Cover Design: Eric Baker

Cover Illustration: Louis Fishauf

Production Artists: Danielle Quan, Deborah Sparck

Other Contributors: Patrick Ames, Rita Amladi, Dean Bernheim, Wendy Bell, Lyn Bishop, Mark Boscacci, Andrea Bruno, Lauren Buchholz, Kurt Clement, Don Craig, Lynn Dalton, Joan Delfino, Laura Dower, Cheryl Elder, Nicole Frees, Erik Gibson, Ron Gross, Steve Guttman, Mark Hamburg, Bruce Hodge, George Holt, Kim Isola, John Knoll, Eve Lynes, Steve Markovich, John Peck, Dayna Porterfield, Dave Pratt, David Rodenborn, Sarah Rosenbaum, Mike Schuster, Cindy Stief, Ed Svoboda, Paul Towner, Karen Winguth

Photographers: Luanne S. Cohen (pp. 24, 58, 66, 70, 78, 94), Disc Imagery (pp. 32, 60), D'Pix Folio 1 (pp. 52, 58, 68, 70), Faith Echtermeyer (p. 33), Curtis Fukuda (pp. 24, 26, 66, 74, 78), Bruce Hodge (pp. 66, 72, 74, 78, 92), Lisa Jeans (pp. 28, 30, 32, 36, 66, 90, 92), Paul C. Jeans (p. 32), Steve Krongard (p. 90), Doug Menuez (pp. 83, 90), Chris Wilson (p. 32)

Contents

Introduction

For decades, graphic designers, illustrators and photographers have used certain techniques to enhance their work. The airbrush is used to simulate shadows; black-and-white photographs are hand-colored using special oil paints; contour shading and texture are added with pen and ink. Often the techniques involve several steps and many different types of tools. These methods have become time-honored traditions for professional artists.

As the computer becomes a standard tool in many professional studios, new methods are being developed to achieve similar results with this tool. The computer can be used to perform some of the more tedious, exacting tasks, such as drawing round-corner boxes and measuring columns evenly. In addition, many time-consuming tasks that have been quite expensive for clients in the past can now be performed very quickly.

Design Essentials tells you how to produce traditional graphic and photographic effects using Adobe software programs. Unlike many computer graphics books, the book does not set out to describe how to use a software program; instead it is a quick how-to reference for artists familiar with the basic features of the Adobe programs.

The techniques included in Design Essentials were collected and developed over the course of a year; many people — both within and outside of Adobe Systems — have contributed to the book. Each procedure and piece of sample art has been tested extensively and proofed on a variety of printers and imagesetters. In addition, Design Essentials includes numerous tips on working efficiently with Adobe software. These tips are marked with the ↝ symbol throughout the book.

Finally, while Design Essentials was created using Adobe software on the Macintosh® computer, most of the techniques in this book can be used with any computer that runs the Adobe software. If you're using the programs on a computer other than the Macintosh, see the Quick Reference Cards provided with your programs for the alternative keyboard shortcuts.

1 Working Efficiently

Setting up your system

Working efficiently in Adobe Illustrator

Working efficiently in Adobe Photoshop

Working efficiently

The time it takes Adobe Photoshop™ or Adobe Illustrator™ to open or save a file, send a file to the printer, or refresh the screen after performing an operation is a measure of the program's "performance." While performance is in part determined by the type of computer and the amount of computer memory you have, many other factors affect performance dramatically. These factors include how you have set up your software, the size of your file, the complexity of the file, and how you perform certain tasks. This section provides guidelines for improving performance and minimizing both the size and the complexity of your files. It also provides workarounds for working with large and complex files and general tips for working efficiently in both programs.

Setting up your system

How you set up your system can dramatically affect performance. For Adobe Illustrator files running under Macintosh® System 6, the amount of memory available for tasks is the same as the amount of available RAM; Adobe Photoshop and Macintosh System 7 also have the capability of using *virtual memory* — hard disk space that can be used for temporary storage of data when RAM is insufficient. For this reason, you can improve performance of both programs by increasing the amount of RAM, while faster disk drives improve performance only if your system uses virtual memory. In addition, you can improve performance by using the following guidelines.

Increase memory allotment. If you are using a Macintosh, increase the amount of memory you have allotted to the application in the Get Info window. If you are using System 7 and have more than 8MB of RAM, turn on 32-bit addressing before increasing the memory allotment. For Photoshop files, increasing the memory allotment to approximately five times the file size will eliminate the need to use virtual memory, and so will significantly speed processing time. With Photoshop, it also helps to turn off the RAM cache in the Control Panel (with System 6) or set the Disk cache in the Memory Control Panel to its lowest setting (with System 7).

Take full advantage of virtual memory. If your system uses virtual memory and you have more than one disk drive, make sure that you have assigned virtual memory to the fastest disk drive with the most free space (for Photoshop, three to five times the file size is recommended for the virtual memory disk). If you are running Photoshop under System 7, turn off virtual memory. If performance still seems slow, try defragmenting the disk using a utility such as Norton Utilities™ or SUM™.

Increase the size of the Adobe Type Manager™ font cache. If you're working with type, you can significantly speed up processing by increasing the size of the font cache in the Adobe Type Manager™ (ATM™) Control Panel. A larger font cache lets you store more font sizes in memory so that ATM doesn't have to rebuild them each time the screen is redrawn. It also enables ATM to generate large sizes that otherwise display as jagged characters. A font cache setting of 320 is sufficient for most projects.

Set up your fonts carefully. Use a font management utility like Suitcase™ or Master Juggler™ to help manage your fonts and to create font suitcases. Because ATM can generate any size typeface from a single font size, be sure that you keep only one size of each type style in your suitcases.

Keep the Clipboard clear of large amounts of data. Images and objects on the Clipboard are stored in RAM and can therefore significantly affect performance. If you have data on the Clipboard from a previous cut and paste operation, select just a few pixels of the image you have open, and copy it (⌘C) to replace the Clipboard data.

Working efficiently in Adobe Illustrator

Because the results of most Illustrator operations are displayed only in Preview Illustration view, most performance issues for Illustrator are directly related to previewing artwork (if not to printing and saving the file). Once you have set up your system for maximum efficiency, you can minimize the time it takes to preview and print by simplifying the complexity of your files and by working around complex paths and images whenever possible.

Preview selectively. If your file is large or complex, you can dramatically speed up previewing either by using the Preview Selection command (⌘-Option-Y) or by hiding the objects you don't need to preview. (To hide all but the selected objects, press ⌘-Option-3.)

Preview without patterns and placed images. When possible, turn off the Show Placed Images and Preview and Print Patterns options in the Preferences dialog box. Remember to turn the Preview and Print Patterns option back on before you print.

Work with two windows open. You can often avoid having to switch back and forth between two views of an illustration by working with two windows open. For example, if you've magnified an image for detail work, choose the New Window command from the Window menu, and display the image at its full size in the second window. You can also use a second window to display an image in Preview Illustration mode while you work in the first window in Artwork Only mode.

Use ⌘-period [.] to cancel previewing. In many cases, a partial preview gives you the information you need to go on with your work. Once Illustrator has started redrawing the screen in Preview mode, you can cancel at any time to return immediately to Artwork mode.

Delete unused patterns and custom colors. In general, it's good practice to delete any patterns and custom colors you are no longer using before you save or print the file. To do this, open the Patterns or Custom Color dialog box, click the Select All Unused button, and click Delete. Because the program deletes all patterns or custom colors not used in the active file, it's important to make sure that you've closed all other files before performing this operation.

Simplify paths. Complex paths — including masks, compound paths, and paths with very many anchor points — can slow processing and cause printing problems. The Flatness setting in the Paint Style dialog box determines the length, in pixels, of the straight line segments used to approximate a curve. You can simplify complex paths by increasing the Flatness setting: for low-resolution devices, a setting of 3 is recommended; for high-resolution devices, a setting of 8 is recommended.

Split paths. Another way to simplify paths is to split them. You can do this by selecting the Split Long Paths option in the Preferences dialog box and entering the resolution of the printer you are using. The program then splits complex paths based on what the printer's memory can handle. (See the user guide for more information on this option.) The Split Long Paths option does not work, however, on stroked paths or on compound paths; to simplify these paths, select the path and split it manually using the scissors tool.

Remove the EPSF Riders program from the program folder. The Riders file lets you modify Adobe Illustrator files at print time using the PostScript™ language code. If you aren't using this file, move it into a folder other than the folder containing the Adobe Illustrator application.

Working efficiently in Adobe Photoshop

Because Adobe Photoshop files can be very large, the key to optimizing performance in Photoshop is finding ways to decrease the size of your files. Once you've done everything you can to decrease file size, you can avoid many performance problems by working on parts of the file individually or by performing certain tasks on smaller, temporary versions of the file. As with Adobe Illustrator, make sure that you have set up your system for maximum efficiency according to the guidelines at the beginning of this section.

Experiment on a low-resolution version of the file. Often, you can save a lot of time by creating a version of your file at 72 dots per inch and making initial edits and color corrections to this version. (You can also change the file's dimensions to decrease file size.) Be sure to save the copy of the file under a different name so that you don't inadvertently replace the original. Once you've figured out exactly what features and dialog box values give you the results you want, open the original file and repeat the steps. If you're adjusting color, you can save the dialog box settings you use for the low-resolution version and then load them with the original file open.

Save selections. Get in the habit of saving complex selections to channels until you have finished editing a file. This lets you load the selection at any time so that you can easily readjust the area without reselecting. If you have a lot of selections, use Calculate/Duplicate to copy them to another file so that they don't increase the size of the file you are working on.

Make complex selections in Gray Scale mode. Because a grayscale image is one-third the size of an RGB image, you can save processing time by making complex selections on a grayscale version of the image, saving the selection to a new channel, and then using the Calculate/Duplicate command to copy the selection into a new channel of the original image. You can also boost the contrast of the grayscale image to make it easier to select shapes of different colors.

Apply filters to channels individually. Some Photoshop filters work in RAM only and do not use virtual memory. If you're having problems running a filter on a color image, try applying the filter to the color channels of the image individually (with the Wave filter, be sure to turn off the Random Start Phase option in the Wave dialog box). Remember that in an RGB image, each channel is one-third the size of the file; in a CMYK image, each channel is one-fourth the size of the file.

Work with two windows open. As with Adobe Illustrator files, you can use the New Window command to avoid having to switch back and forth between views of a file. For example, you can work on a magnified version of an image while viewing the entire image in a second window, or make color corrections to an image while viewing the results in both the composite color channel and an individual color channel of the image.

Create a customized color palette. To save time choosing colors, create a customized color palette for the file. Open a blank color file (use a resolution of 72 dots per inch and a height and width of not more than 200 pixels to keep the file size small); then paint in the colors you want to use, or use the technique described on page 36 to create a full-color spectrum. You can then use the eyedropper tool to sample colors from this file just as you do from the color palette window.

Use the shortcuts. As with Adobe Illustrator, you can save a lot of time by learning the shortcuts for accessing tools and commands. These are especially useful for operations that you perform all the time such as magnifying (double-click the hand tool to fit an image in the window; double-click the zoom tool to display an image at actual size) and filling a selection with color (on the Macintosh, use Option-Delete to fill with the foreground color and Delete to fill with the background color).

2 Lines and Perspective

Dashed line effects

Software needed: Adobe Illustrator 3

You can generate a variety of useful and decorative effects by varying the dash patterns of your lines and then layering the lines. The following charts provide recipes for just a few examples. To create any of the single-line effects, simply select any line in Adobe Illustrator, open the Paint dialog box (⌘I), and enter the values shown here. To create the layered-line effects, Option-select the line (this ensures that the entire line is selected) and paint it using the values shown in the first row of the recipe; then copy the line, choose Paste In Front (⌘F), and paint the copy using the values in the next row of the recipe. Repeat this procedure until all layers have been created and painted; then preview the results (⌘Y). When you have achieved the effect you want, group the lines (⌘G). Experiment with your own dash patterns to create other effects.

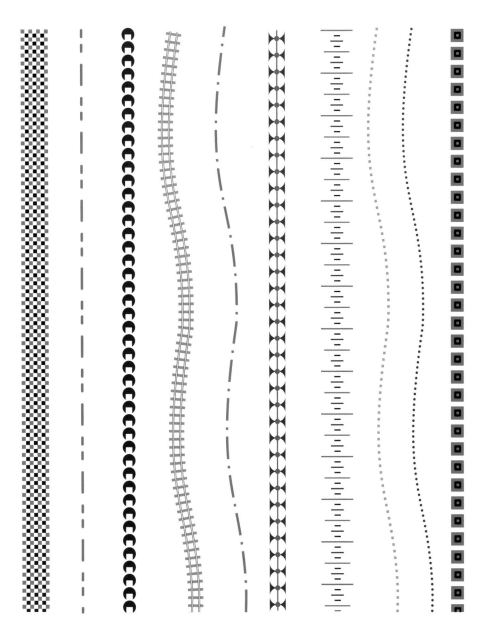

SINGLE LINES	STROKE COLOR	STROKE WIDTH (IN POINTS)	LINE CAP STYLE	DASH PATTERN
	100%	2	ROUND	0, 2
	100%	2	ROUND	0, 4
	100%	2	ROUND	0, 6
	100%	2	ROUND	0, 10
	100%	2	ROUND	20, 16
	100%	2	ROUND	0, 4, 0, 4, 5, 4
	100%	2	ROUND	0, 4, 4, 8, 4, 4
	100%	2	ROUND	8, 4, 0, 4, 8, 10
	100%	2	ROUND	20, 8, 0, 8
	100%	2	ROUND	20, 7, 7, 7
	100%	2	ROUND	5, 6, 5, 10, 15, 10
	100%	2	PROJECTING	0, 5
	100%	2	PROJECTING	0, 10
	100%	2	PROJECTING	15, 5
	100%	2	PROJECTING	15, 7, 0, 7
	100%	2	PROJECTING	20, 7, 7, 7

BUTT   ROUND   PROJECTING

SINGLE LINES	STROKE COLOR	STROKE WIDTH (IN POINTS)	LINE CAP STYLE	DASH PATTERN
	100%	4	BUTT	0.3, 8
	100%	8	BUTT	0.3, 4
	100%	12	BUTT	0.3, 2
	100%	16	BUTT	0.3, 2
	100%	10	BUTT	4, 3
	100%	18	BUTT	3, 4
	100%	12	BUTT	0.3, 2, 0.3, 6, 5, 6
	100%	15	BUTT	2, 4, 10

LAYERED LINES (VALUES SHOWN BY LAYER)	STROKE COLOR	STROKE WIDTH (IN POINTS)	LINE CAP STYLE	DASH PATTERN
	100%	5	BUTT	1, 3
	100%	10	BUTT	1, 7
	100%	20	BUTT	1, 15
	100%	25	BUTT	1, 31
	20%	25	BUTT	0.6, 2
	40%	20	BUTT	0.6, 2
	60%	15	BUTT	0.6, 2
	80%	10	BUTT	0.6, 2
	100%	5	BUTT	0.6, 2
	100%	25	BUTT	2, 2
	80%	20	BUTT	2, 2
	60%	15	BUTT	2, 2
	40%	10	BUTT	2, 2
	20%	5	BUTT	2, 2
	100%	20	BUTT	SOLID
	WHITE	15	BUTT	3, 5
	100%	10	BUTT	SOLID
	100%	17.5	BUTT	2.5, 2.5
	WHITE	12.5	BUTT	SOLID
	100%	7.5	BUTT	2.5, 2.5
	WHITE	2.5	BUTT	SOLID

 BUTT ⬭ ROUND ▭ PROJECTING

LAYERED LINES (VALUES SHOWN BY LAYER)	STROKE COLOR	STROKE WIDTH (IN POINTS)	LINE CAP STYLE	DASH PATTERN
	100%	21	BUTT	3, 3
	100%	15	BUTT	SOLID
	WHITE	15	BUTT	3, 3
	WHITE	9	BUTT	SOLID
	100%	9	BUTT	3, 3
	100%	3	BUTT	SOLID
	WHITE	3	BUTT	3, 3
	100%	13.5	BUTT	2.5, 10
	100%	7.5	BUTT	SOLID
	WHITE	7.5	BUTT	2.5, 2.5, 3.5, 0, 4, 0
	100%	2.5	BUTT	SOLID
	WHITE	2.5	BUTT	5, 2.5, 5, 0
	100%	7.5	BUTT	2.5, 7.5
	100%	5	BUTT	5, 5
	100%	2.5	BUTT	7.5, 2.5
	100%	10	ROUND	0, 10
	WHITE	5	ROUND	0, 10
	100%	15	ROUND	0, 15
	WHITE	15	BUTT	1.5, 2.25, 1.5, 9.75
	100%	10	ROUND	0, 10
	WHITE	5	BUTT	5, 5
	100%	12.5	BUTT	SOLID
	WHITE	12.5	ROUND	0, 12.5
	100%	4	ROUND	0, 6.25
	WHITE	4	ROUND	0, 12.5
	100%	1	BUTT	SOLID
	100%	12.5	BUTT	7.5, 2.5, 2.5, 2.5
	WHITE	7.5	BUTT	5, 10
	100%	5	ROUND	0, 15
	100%	12	BUTT	2, 4
	100%	7	BUTT	SOLID
	WHITE	6	BUTT	SOLID
	100%	5	BUTT	SOLID
	WHITE	4	BUTT	SOLID
	100%	4	BUTT	2, 4
	100%	10	PROJECTING	0, 13.5
	WHITE	5	PROJECTING	0, 13.5
	100%	2.5	PROJECTING	0, 13.5
	100%	15	BUTT	15, 2.5
	WHITE	10	BUTT	12.5, 5
	100%	5	BUTT	2.5, 15*
	100%	2.5	BUTT	10, 7.5

*move line down 2.5 points

Shapes with multiple outlines

Software needed: Adobe Illustrator 3, Adobe Type Manager, and Type 1 Fonts

You can create shapes with multiple outlines in Adobe Illustrator by stacking copies of the shapes on top of each other and stroking them with different colors. The last copy of the shape on the stack is filled with a color and no stroke value, so that only the outlines of the copies underneath appear around it. This process is analogous to overlaying increasingly smaller pieces of paper — each larger piece of paper creates a frame around the smaller piece on top of it, giving a final effect of multiple borders, or outlines.

Before you begin, you'll probably want to determine the best stroke widths for your shape or type outline. Remember that when you stroke a path, Adobe Illustrator creates the border from the center of the path — this means that a stroke value of 6 points will create only a 3-point border outside the path. The stroke value of each consecutive layer determines the width of the border beneath it; for example, a 4-point stroke on top of a 6-point stroke will give you a border of 1 point ($^6/_2$ - $^4/_2$).

Finally, when stroking type, it's important to copy an unstroked version of the type on top of the stroked type to maintain the integrity of the orginal letterform.

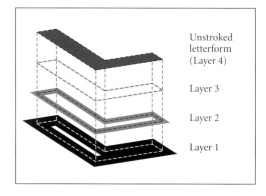

Unstroked letterform (Layer 4)

Layer 3

Layer 2

Layer 1

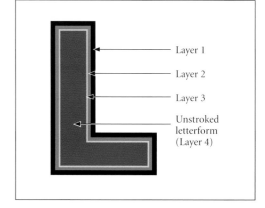

Layer 1

Layer 2

Layer 3

Unstroked letterform (Layer 4)

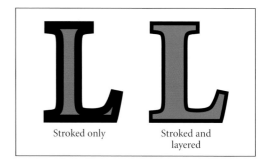

Stroked only

Stroked and layered

1. To create type with multiple outlines, use the type tool to create the word or letters you want to outline, and kern if necessary. If you are working with shapes other than type, skip to step 3.

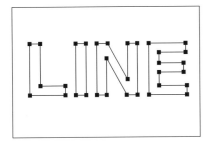

2. Select the text with the selection tool, and choose Create Outlines from the Type menu. Remember that choosing Create Outlines turns the type into paths that can no longer be edited using the type tool. Group the letters (⌘G) to prevent them from being moved or transformed individually.

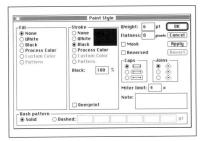

3. With the outlines selected, choose Style from the Paint menu (⌘I). Fill with None and stroke with the color you want to use for the outermost outline. Remember that the stroke width you should use depends on the size of your object and how wide you want each border (in this example, we used a 6-point stroke for the outermost outline of an 54-point letterform).

4. Preview (⌘Y) to check your work.

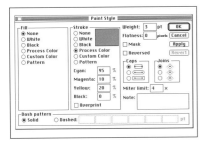

5. Copy the selected letterforms (⌘C) and choose Paste in Front (⌘F). This places the copy directly on top of the first outline. Fill this second layer with None, and stroke it with a thinner stroke than used for the first layer (we used a 3-point stroke for the second layer) and a different color.

6. Preview (⌘Y) to check your work.

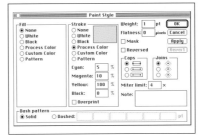

7. Choose Paste in Front (⌘F) to paste the letters from the Clipboard again; this creates a third layer. Fill this outline with None and stroke it with a third color. (We used a 1-point stroke.)

8. Preview (⌘Y) to check your work.

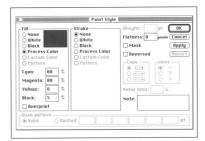

9. When you have created a layer for each outline you want, choose Paste in Front (⌘F) once more to paste the final layer; with type, this step is necessary to retain the shape of the original letterform. Fill this layer with the color you want and stroke it with None.

10. Preview (⌘Y) to check your work.

Creating offset outlines

Software needed: Adobe Illustrator 3

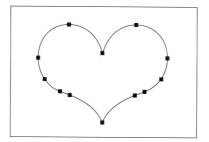

1. Create the shape you want to use, select it, and group it (⌘G).

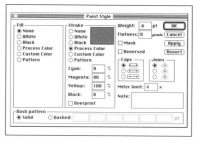

2. Open the Paint Style dialog box (⌘I) and stroke the shape.

3. Preview the shape (⌘Y) to check your work.

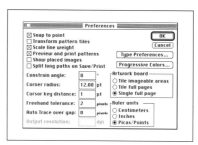

4. In the Preferences dialog box (⌘K), set the Ruler Units to Picas/Points, and turn on the Snap to Point option.

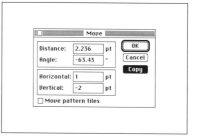

5. With the object still selected, open the Move dialog box. (Option-click the selection tool in the toolbox to open the Move dialog box.) Specify a distance and an angle for the move; for most offset outlines, a distance 1.5 to 2 times the shape's line weight produces the best effect.

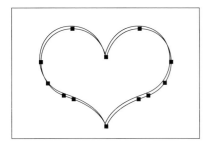

6. Click Copy to create an offset duplicate of the shape.

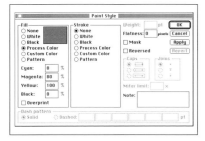

7. Open the Paint Style dialog box (⌘I), and fill the copy.

8. Preview the artwork (⌘Y). If you are satisfied with the effect, group the shapes (⌘G). This defines the shapes as a single unit, and prevents them from being moved or transformed separately.

❧ *Using the cursor keys for precise movements*

Use the cursor keys on your keyboard to move objects by the increments set in the Cursor Key Distance field in the Preferences dialog box (⌘K). This is especially useful when you need to move anchor points or objects temporarily and then move them back into position. In the example shown here, the cursor keys are used to help turn a compound path (in this case, a letterform) into a simple closed path for easier previewing and printing. (See "Working Efficiently" for more information on simplifying paths.)

1. Use scissors to cut both paths where they will be joined.

2. Move upper endpoints with cursor keys to separate.

3. Join corresponding points of each path.

4. Return points to original position with cursor keys.

❧ *Changing colors automatically*

Sometimes after you've painted an image, you want to change certain colors in the artwork. This can be time-consuming if you've painted the objects with process color mixes. It's good practice to specify your process color mixes as custom colors using the Custom Color dialog box. This lets you easily repaint objects by changing the CMYK values for the custom colors. If you know the artwork eventually will be separated as process colors, use Adobe Separator™ to convert the custom colors to process colors.

Create your custom colors and use the Paint Style dialog box to paint your artwork. It can be helpful to name the colors after the objects.

To create a new color version, choose Save As from the File menu. Save the file with a suffix such as *.version2*. With only the second file open, open the Custom Color dialog box under the Paint menu. Select one of the colors and change its CMYK values.

Continue to change the color percentages for each custom color that you want to alter. It is a good idea to add a number 2 at the end of the custom color name to keep track of the different color versions. If you have two files open with the same custom color names but with different color values, the file opened most recently will override the color values of the file opened first.

Once you have finished changing the color values, click OK. Preview the image (⌘Y) to view the color change.

Creating three-dimensional boxes

Software needed: Adobe Illustrator 3

The following three procedures describe how to create three-dimensional artwork in Adobe Illustrator. This technique describes how to use Adobe Illustrator's precision tools to create isometric, axonometric, dimetric, and trimetric views from your two-dimensional artwork. The chart at the end of this technique provides the precise values needed for each type of three-dimensional drawing.

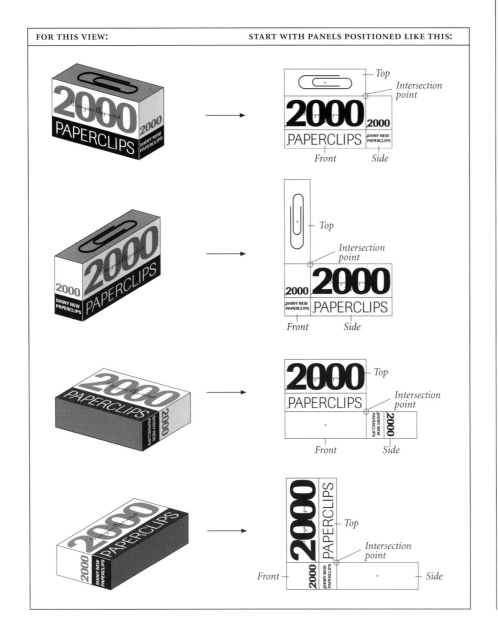

FOR THIS VIEW:	START WITH PANELS POSITIONED LIKE THIS:

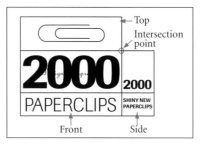

1. Create a flat view of your package, and group each panel (⌘G). Using the examples shown on the left of this page, choose the three panels you need to produce a perspective view, and position them as indicated. The top, front, and side panels will be scaled, sheared, and rotated using the intersection of the three panels as the point of origin.

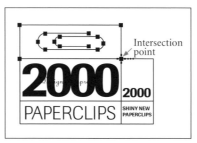

2. Select the top panel; then choose the scale tool, and Option-click the intersection point to set the point of origin and open the Scale dialog box.

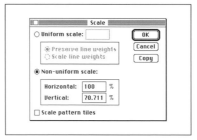

3. Click the Non-uniform Scale option, and scale the panel vertically, using the Vertical value shown for your chosen view in the chart on the facing page. (The Horizontal value should be 100%.) In this example, we entered the values for the trimetric 2 view.

4. With the top panel still selected, choose the shear tool, and Option-click the intersection point. Shear the panel along the horizontal axis, using the value indicated in the chart.

5. Now you will rotate the top panel so that it appears to go back in space. Choose the rotate tool, and Option-click the intersection point. Enter the rotate value indicated in the chart, and click OK.

6. Repeat steps 2-5 for the front panel. Be sure to substitute the correct numbers from the chart. For the correct results, it's important to follow steps 2-5 in order, first scaling, then shearing, and then rotating the panel, using the intersection point as the point of origin.

7. Repeat steps 2-5 for the side panel, using the next set of numbers from the chart.

8. Preview the artwork (⌘Y). If the panel is stroked, zoom in very close on the corner joints and check to see if the corners extend past the intersection point, as shown in this illustration. Identify which panels have this problem.

9. Using the direct-selection tool, select the problem panel edges, open the Paint dialog box (⌘I), and choose the rounded Join option. Click OK. Preview (⌘Y) to check your work.

10. To enhance the three-dimensional effect of the artwork, paint the panels with slightly different shades and tints. In this example, we lightened the colors on the top panel and darkened the colors on the side panel.

VIEW	A	B	COMMON NAME	FACE	VERTICAL SCALE	HORIZ. SHEAR	ROTATE
				TOP	100.000%	0°	-45°
	45°	45°	AXONOMETRIC	FRONT	70.711%	-45°	-45°
				SIDE	70.711%	45°	45°
				TOP	86.602%	30°	-30°
	30°	30°	ISOMETRIC	FRONT	86.602%	-30°	-30°
				SIDE	86.602%	30°	30°
				TOP	96.592%	15°	-15°
	15°	60°	DIMETRIC	FRONT	96.592%	-15°	-15°
				SIDE	50.000%	60°	60°
				TOP	86.602%	30°	-15°
	15°	45°	TRIMETRIC 1	FRONT	96.592%	-15°	-15°
				SIDE	70.711%	45°	45°
				TOP	70.711%	45°	-15°
	15°	30°	TRIMETRIC 2	FRONT	96.592%	-15°	-15°
				SIDE	86.602%	30°	30°

Creating a three-dimensional pie chart

Software needed: Adobe Illustrator 3

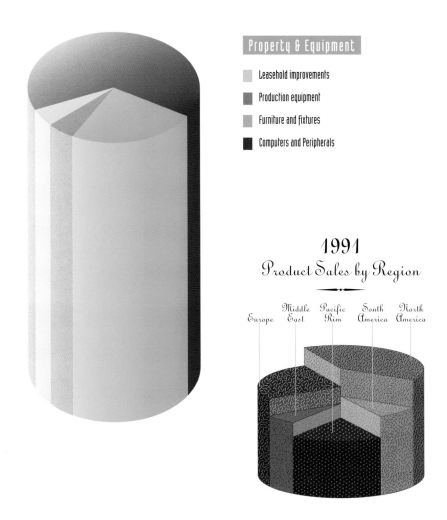

Property & Equipment

- Leasehold improvements
- Production equipment
- Furniture and fixtures
- Computers and Peripherals

1991
Product Sales by Region

Europe · Middle East · Pacific Rim · South America · North America

Left: After making the three-dimensional chart, we made each pie piece into a mask. We then grouped each mask with a different blend.
Right: To paint this chart, we began with pattern tiles from Adobe Collector's Edition™: Patterns and Textures. Each pattern tile was painted and saved as a custom pattern. To create the effect of shadows, we used the same pattern tiles, painted with slightly darker colors.

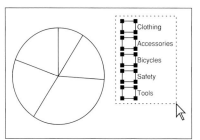

1. Create a pie chart in Adobe Illustrator. (See the *Adobe Illustrator Tutorial* for step-by-step instructions on creating a pie chart.) Make sure that the Snap to Point option is turned on in the Preferences dialog box (⌘K). Once you are sure that your data is final, make a back-up copy of the chart; then remove the graph "key" using the direct-selection tool.

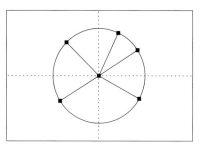

2. For the best results, no side of any pie wedge should be horizontal or vertical. To achieve this, choose Show Rulers (⌘R) and drag guides from the rulers that intersect the center of the pie; then select the pie and rotate it so that each guide intersects the center of two pieces as much as possible. Remove the guides when you have finished.

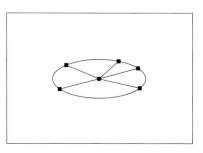

3. Reselect the pie. To create an illusion of depth, select the scale tool and Option-click the center point of the pie. In the Scale dialog box, select Non-uniform, and enter a Horizontal value of 100% and a Vertical value of 40%. Click OK.

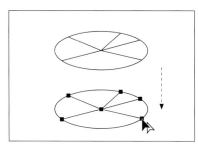

4. To create the bottom of the three-dimensional pie, use the selection tool to begin dragging the pie downward; then hold down the Option and Shift keys to make a copy and constrain its movement. When the new pie is directly below the original, release the mouse button and then the Option and Shift keys. Ungroup both pies (⌘U) twice.

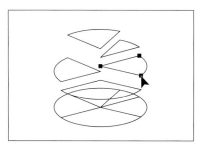

5. To stagger the pie pieces, select one piece of the upper pie, and drag it downward while holding the Shift key to constrain its movement. Repeat this step for the remaining upper pieces until you are satisfied with the height of each piece.

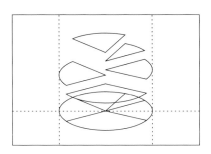

6. To help you create straight vertical edges between the top and bottom of the three-dimensional pie, drag a horizontal guide to the center point of the lower pie. Place vertical guides where the horizontal guide meets the left and right edges of the pie.

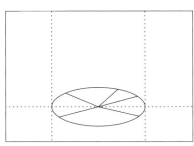

7. You can now remove the unwanted segments of the lower pie. It is easier to do this if you first select the upper pie pieces and hide them (⌘3). Hiding objects is a good way to protect artwork when making changes or cleaning up your file.

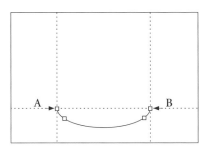

8. Ungroup each piece in the lower pie (⌘U) twice. Use the scissors tool to cut the pie at points A and B, as shown in the illustration. Delete all segments except the bottom curve. This segment becomes the bottom of your three-dimensional pie chart.

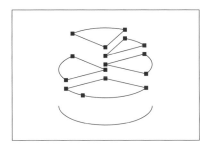

9. Choose Show All from the Arrange menu (⌘4) to redisplay the hidden segments.

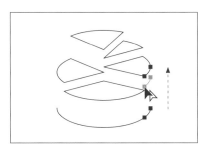

10. Select the rightmost segment of the new curve, and choose Bring to Front (⌘=). Begin dragging the inside endpoint upward; then press the Shift and Option keys. When the cursor "snaps to" the corresponding endpoint of the rightmost pie piece, release the mouse button and then the keys. Repeat this process for each segment of the bottom curve.

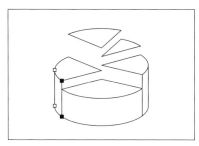

11. For each segment you have just copied, select the corresponding upper and lower endpoints of the segment, and join them (⌘J). If you have trouble selecting points, bring the shape you are working with to the front layer of the artwork (⌘=). Repeat this step for the remaining front pie pieces. Group each shape individually.

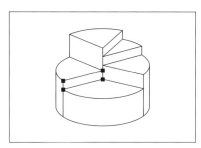

12. With the pen tool, draw the rectangular sides of the pie pieces by clicking directly on the corner points. Group each new rectangle side.

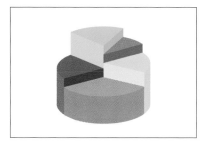

13. Paint the top and sides of each pie piece a unique color, pattern, or percentage of color; then preview (⌘Y) to check your work . If you want to further embellish this chart using Adobe Photoshop (see page 52), make sure that the segments are not stroked to allow for cleaner selections.

❧ *Previewing Adobe Illustrator files in other applications*

To get a quick black-and-white preview version of an Adobe Illustrator image into another application, you can use the Clipboard to bring a PICT version of the image into the other application. While running in Multifinder® or under System 7, select the Illustrator image or object you want to export and preview. Hold down the Option key and copy the image (⌘C). This places a black-and-white PICT version of the image on the Clipboard. You can now paste the image (⌘V) into any application that accepts PICT Clipboard images.

Creating a three-dimensional bar chart

Software needed: Adobe Illustrator 3

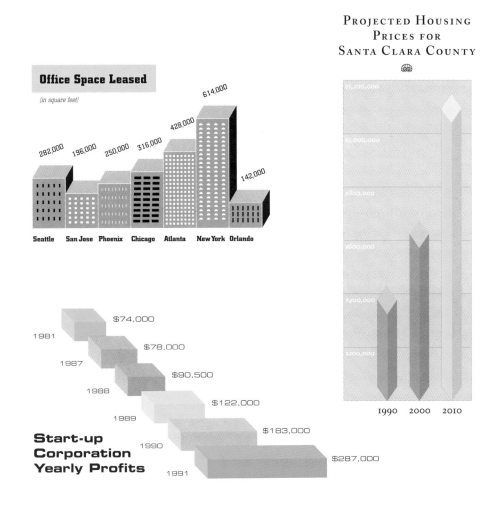

Office Space Leased

(in square feet)

614,000
428,000
282,000 196,000 250,000 316,000 142,000

Seattle   San Jose   Phoenix   Chicago   Atlanta   New York   Orlando

PROJECTED HOUSING
PRICES FOR
SANTA CLARA COUNTY

$1,200,000
$1,000,000
$800,000
$600,000
$400,000
$200,000

1990   2000   2010

$74,000
1981
$78,000
1987
$90,500
1988
$122,000
1989
$183,000
1990
$287,000
1991

**Start-up
Corporation
Yearly Profits**

Top left: Window rectangles were added using the Transform Again command. Typeface: Berthold City®.
Top right: The graph design was created using the rectangle tool with the constrain angle in the Preferences dialog box set at 45°. Typeface: Adobe Caslon™.
Bottom left: Bars were rotated 90° and sheared at a 30° angle. Typeface: Eurostile™.

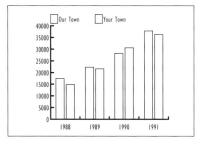

1. Create a grouped or stacked bar chart in Adobe Illustrator. (See the *Adobe Illustrator Tutorial* for step-by-step instructions on creating a bar chart.) Turn on the Snap to Point option in the Preferences dialog box (⌘K).

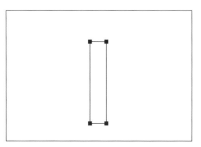

2. Choose the direct-selection tool. Option-click one of the columns in the graph to select it, and copy it to the Clipboard (⌘C).

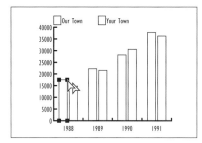

3. Scroll to a blank area of the document and paste the copy of the column from the Clipboard (⌘V); this will be the bounding rectangle of your three-dimensional graph design. Hold down the Command key and the Spacebar and zoom in so you can draw more accurately. Choose the selection tool (⌘Tab).

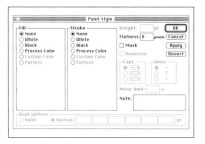

4. Paint the bounding rectangle with a fill and stroke of None; then copy it to the Clipboard (⌘V).

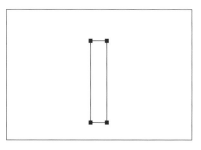

5. To create the face of your three-dimensional graph design, paste another copy of the column directly on top of the bounding rectangle (⌘F). This ensures that the face of the column aligns with the graph tick marks, and makes the graph easier to read. Paint the rectangle with the color you want for the face of your columns (⌘I).

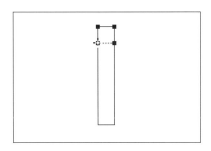

6. Now create a top for the column. With the rectangle still selected, choose the scale tool and Option-click the upper left corner point of the bar. In the Scale dialog box, click Non-uniform and enter a Horizontal value of 100% and a Vertical value of -20%. Click Copy. (You can change the size of the top by adjusting the vertical scale amount.)

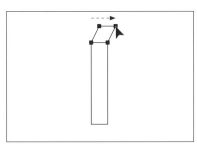

7. Now create an illusion of depth. With the top still selected, choose the shear tool and click the lower left corner point. Position the pointer over the upper right corner point, hold down the Shift key, and drag to the right. When you are satisfied with the shear angle of the top, release the mouse button and then the Shift key. Paint the top of the column (⌘I).

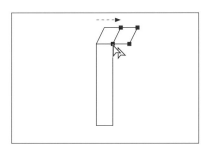

8. Next, create a shape for the side of the bar. With the selection tool, drag the top by the bottom left corner point to the right, holding down the Option and Shift keys to make a copy and to constrain its movement. When the pointer "snaps to" the bottom right corner point of the original, release the mouse button and then the Option and Shift keys.

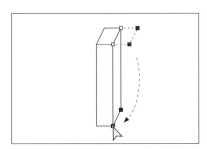

9. Choose the direct-selection tool (⌘Tab). Hold down the Shift key and select only the rightmost anchor points of this new shape. Release the Shift key; then drag the shape by its lower right corner point until it "snaps to" the bottom right corner point of the bar. Paint the side of the column (⌘I).

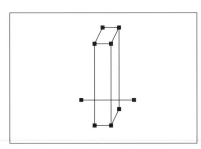

10. So that the column design can be scaled for different *y*-axis values without distorting the design, define a "sliding boundary" — a line below which the design will be scaled. With the pen tool, draw a horizontal line that intersects the column design. (Hold down the Shift key to make sure that the line is perfectly horizontal.) Select the entire design, and group it (⌘G).

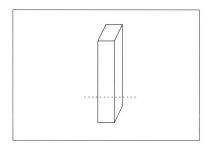

11. Using the direct-selection tool, select the horizontal line and choose Make Guide from the Arrange menu (⌘5). (To check that you've done this correctly, use the selection tool — not the direct-selection tool — to drag the column design; the guide should move with the design.)

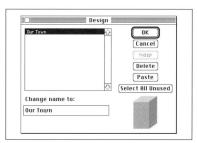

12. With the column design still selected, choose Define Graph Design (⌘-Shift-Option-G), and click New. Name the design, and click OK. You can now use this design in any column graph you create with the graph tool.

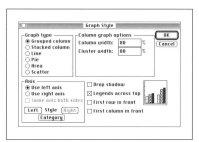

13. Scroll back to the graph and zoom out. Select the graph and choose Use Column Design (⌘-Shift-Option-C). Click the Sliding option under Column Design Type, select the name of your design, and click OK.

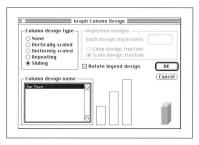

14. To prevent problems in the layering order of the columns, open the Graph Style dialog box (⌘-Shift-Option-S), and make sure the First Column in Front option is not selected.

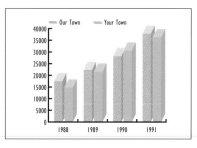

15. Preview (⌘Y) to check your work. If necessary, use the direct-selection tool to adjust the layering of the axis lines. You can also change the paint attributes of individual columns or column sides. If you want to further embellish this chart in Adobe Photoshop (see page 52), make sure that the segments are not stroked to allow for cleaner selections.

Shaded spherical objects

Software needed: Adobe Photoshop 2.0

A water molecule

An ammonia molecule

Top & middle left: A one-inch sphere was created, then copied twice and scaled. Typeface: Helvetica Inserat.
Right: We created the sphere and then scaled it horizontally. We cut the top by selecting it with the elliptical marquee tool and added the red pimento using the paint brush. Highlights were added with the airbrush tool.
Bottom: Before creating the blue sphere, we applied the Add Noise filter to each of the highlight channels (6-9) using the Uniform option and a value of 20. We then created the sphere, selected it, and applied the Gaussian Blur filter using a value of 20. To create the egg shape, we used the Perspective command.

To shade spherical objects, you create multiple shaded rings, starting with the center of the highlighted area. The exact size and positioning of each ring depends on the size of the object you are shading and is essential to producing the proper effect. The example shown here produces the desired results for a sphere that is 200 by 200 pixels (1 inch) at a resolution of 200 pixels per inch. The chart below provides sizes and coordinates for other sphere sizes at this resolution. Notice that the x, y coordinates and the blur amount change incrementally for different sphere sizes. For the best results, do this procedure in CMYK mode; this will help prevent banding when you print.

SIZE		STEPS 5-9	STEP 10	STEP 11	STEP 12
3″ SPHERE (600 x 600 PIXELS)	CIRCLE SIZE (PIXELS)	75 X 75	265 X 265	475 X 475	575 X 575
	X, Y POSITION	-44.6, -44.6	-44.6, -44.6	-39.2, -39.2	-26.3, -26.3
	BLUR RADIUS	20	40	60	25
	FILL OPACITY	10	30	70	85
5″ SPHERE (1000 x 1000 PIXELS)	CIRCLE SIZE (PIXELS)	125 X 125	440 X 440	790 X 790	957 X 957
	X, Y POSITION	-74.5, -74.5	-74.5, -74.5	-65.5, -65.5	-43.6, -43.6
	BLUR RADIUS	34	68	100	42
	FILL OPACITY	10	30	70	85

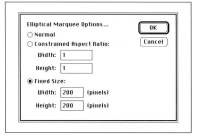

1. Open a new CMYK file (⌘N) at 200 ppi. In the Units Preferences dialog box, change the Ruler Units to points. Choose Show Rulers (⌘R); then drag the ruler origin to where you want the center of the sphere. Double-click the elliptical marquee tool, click Fixed Size, and enter a height and width of 200 pixels. Click OK.

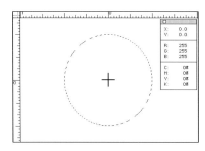

2. Choose Show Info from the Window menu, then hold down the Option key and drag to align the center of the circle on the 0, 0 coordinate. Use the Show Info window to help you position the circle.

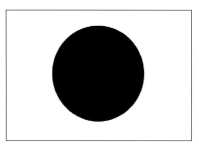

3. Choose Save Selection from the Select menu to save the selection to a new channel (channel #5). Invert this channel by choosing Map and then Invert from the Image menu (⌘I).

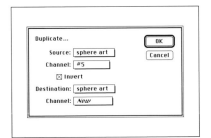

4. Choose Calculate from the Image menu and Duplicate from the submenu. Change the Destination name so that it matches the Source name, click the Invert option, and click OK. This creates an inverted duplicate of channel #5 in a new channel (channel #6).

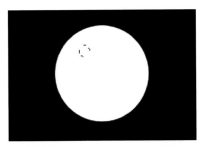

5. To begin shading the sphere, you first create the white spot at the center of the highlighted area. Double-click the elliptical marquee tool, enter Fixed Size values of 25 by 25 pixels, and click OK. Hold down the Option key and drag the circle until both the *x* and *y* coordinates in the Show Info window read -14.8 points.

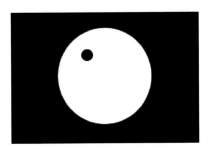

6. Set the foreground color to black by double-clicking the eyedropper tool in the toolbox. Fill the circle with black (Option-Delete); then deselect the circle (⌘D).

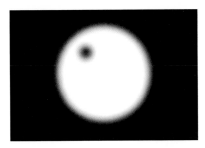

7. From the Filter menu, choose Blur and then Gaussian Blur. Enter 7 for the blur radius, and click OK.

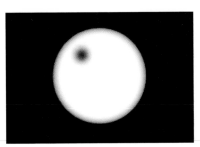

8. Load selection #5; then fill it with black (Option-Delete). This gives the sphere a hard edge. Deselect everything (⌘D).

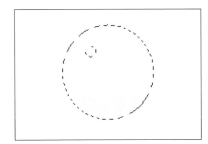

9. Go to the CMYK channel (⌘0), and load selection #6. Choose Show Palette from the Window menu, and select a new foreground color. Choose Fill from the Edit menu, and fill the selection with using an Opacity of 10%; then deselect (⌘D).

10. Return to channel #6 (⌘6) to begin the second ring. Repeat steps 5 through 9 using a Fixed Size value of 85 by 85 pixels and *x* and *y* coordinates of -14.8 in step 5, a Gaussian Blur radius of 15 in step 7, and a fill opacity of 30% in step 9.

11. Repeat these steps to create a third ring using the following values:

Circle size:	155 x 155 pixels
Coordinates:	-13.0, -13.0
Blur radius:	20 pixels
Fill opacity:	70%

12. Create a fourth and final ring using the following values:

Circle size:	190 x 190 pixels
Coordinates:	-8.6, -8.6
Blur radius:	9 pixels
Fill opacity:	85%

13. To compensate for banding, or shade-stepping, apply the Add Noise filter in each CMYK channel, using an Amount of 3 and the Uniform Distribution option. To ensure that the filter affects only the sphere and not the rest of the file, load channel #5 and invert it (⌘I) before applying the filter in each channel. (See page 41 for more information on banding.)

3 Painting and Blending

Creating impressionist effects

Software needed: Adobe Photoshop 2.0

You can use a variety of techniques to give your artwork a painterly, impressionistic look. This procedure describes how to use the Calculate feature to combine a texture image file with a color image file. Using this basic technique, you can apply different Calculate commands and options to achieve an almost limitless number of effects. The Calculate feature lets you combine different channels or single-channel images using a variety of comparison strategies. You can also use the Calculate/Duplicate command to create a quick, unsaved copy of an image channel for experimenting with different features and effects. Once you've become accustomed to the Calculate feature, you'll find yourself using it all the time.

1. Open a grayscale image or convert a color image to grayscale using the Mode menu. Because you will be using a grayscale and a color version of the same image, save this file with a suffix of *.gray*.

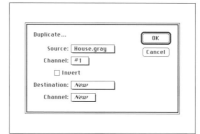

2. Select Calculate from the Image menu and Duplicate from the submenu. Duplicate the grayscale image to a new file. This gives you an unsaved copy of the file to experiment with, and leaves the original image file intact.

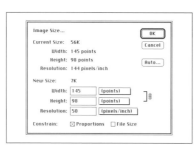

3. With the duplicated image window active, choose Image Size from the Image menu. Write down the current width, height, and resolution for later reference. Be sure the File Size Constrain option is unselected, and reduce the resolution to 30-50 pixels per inch. This will allow you to paint large areas of the image very quickly.

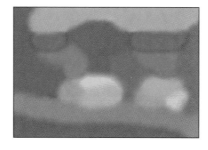

4. Convert the image to RGB mode. Choose Show Palette from the Window menu, and select a color. Double-click the paint brush tool in the toolbox, choose a large brush size, and begin painting over the grayscale image. Paint the large or important shapes in your composition. This file will define the basic colors and color areas in the final image.

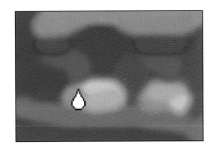

5. When you've finished painting, use the blur tool to soften the hard edges. Double-click the blur tool, choose a large brush, and drag to blur the edges of the image where two colors meet.

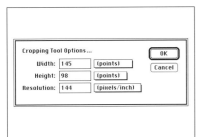

6. Double-click the cropping tool, and enter the values that you recorded in step 3; then select the entire image and crop. Because resampling in step 3 may have changed the dimensions of the file by one pixel, you must use the cropping tool to ensure that the color and grayscale files are exactly the same size and resolution. Save this file with the suffix *.color*.

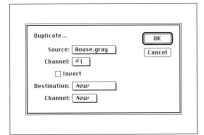

7. Using the Calculate function, duplicate the grayscale file again to a new file. Save this file with the suffix *.texture*. This file will define the texture of the final image.

8. Now create the impressionist texture that you will eventually combine with the color file. Choose Stylize from the Filter menu and Pointillize from the submenu. In the dialog box, enter a value between 3 and 5, and click OK.

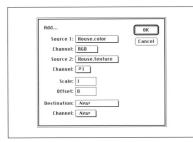

9. To combine the *.texture* and *.color* files, choose Add from the Calculate submenu, and select the two filenames in the Source boxes. You can add the files in either order; however, make sure that the *.color* file channel is RGB and the *.texture* file channel is #1. Leave the Scale and Offset values at their defaults, and click OK.

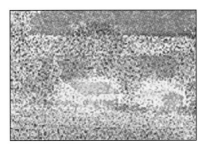

10. The two files are combined in a new file. If you are satisfied with the results, save the file with a suffix of *.impress;* if not, close the file and repeat steps 8 and 9 using different values. To make the new file darker, use a Scale value below 2.0 (a value of 2.0 averages the color values of the two files); you can make it even darker by entering a positive value in the Offset field.

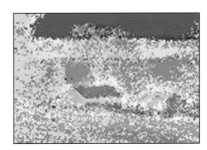

Variation: Instead of using the Pointillize filter in step 8, use the Posterize command under the Image menu (⌘J) to posterize the image to 3 levels; then apply the Diffuse filter several times to create the desired texture. (In this example, the Diffuse filter was applied three times.) You can also invert the texture image to reverse the shadow and highlight areas.

Use the Add command to combine the two files in a new file. In this example, we used a Scale value of 1 and an Offset value of 0.

Using the Calculate feature

The Calculate feature is a very powerful tool that lets you combine channels in the same or different files based on the color values in each file. Because all of the Calculate commands function by comparing the color values in the file pixel by pixel, the files must have *exactly* the same dimensions, resolution, and file size. If they are off by even a single pixel, you won't be able to select the files in the Calculate dialog boxes.

If you temporarily change the resolution of a file, as in this procedure, it's a good idea to use the cropping tool rather than the Image Size command to restore the image to its original file size. This is because when the resolution is changed, the Image Size command may add a pixel to the height or width to maintain a whole number of pixels. Using the cropping command to restore the original file size ensures that any extra pixels are deleted from the file.

More impressionist techniques

Software needed: Adobe Photoshop 2.0

Smudge tool

1. Open the file you want to alter. Save the file with a filename suffix of *.smudged;* this preserves the original file in case you want to create several variations.

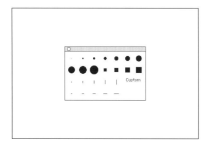

2. Choose Show Brushes from the Window menu to open the brush palette. Keep this palette open as you may want to change brush sizes several times during the painting session.

3. Select the smudge tool. Begin smudging a shape in the direction of its significant lines, or "grain." For example, if you are smudging grass, smudge in the direction the blades point. Change direction for each different shape. For large areas, choose a larger brush. For delicate, detailed areas, use a smaller brush.

4. You can also adjust the intensity of the smudge effect by double-clicking the tool in the toolbox and changing the Pressure value. To correct an area, use the rubber stamp tool with the Revert option to restore the area, and try smudging again.

Impressionist tool

1. Open the file you want to alter. Save the file with a filename suffix of *.impress;* this preserves the original file in case you want to create several variations. It's a good idea to try this technique on a small image first. Because the impressionist tool paints with the last saved version of the file, you won't save the file until you have finished painting.

2. Now erase the image and create a color background, or "canvas," that will show through the spaces of your impressionist painting. Choose the color from the color palette or use the eyedropper tool to select a color from the image (white or black also work well). Choose Select All (⌘A), and press Delete. Fill with the color (Option-Delete), and deselect (⌘D).

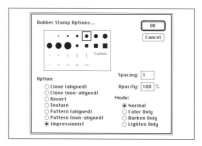

3. Double-click the rubber stamp tool, and select the Impressionist option. Select a brush size; in most cases, medium to small brushes give the best results.

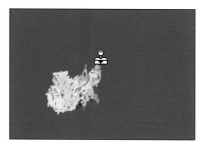

4. Begin painting with the impressionist tool. If you created a background in step 2, leave some space between your brush strokes.

5. Experiment with different brush sizes. To make more of the background show through, change the Opacity value in the Rubber Stamp Options dialog box. Save the file only after you have finished painting completely.

Pointillize filter

1. Open the file you want to alter. Save the file with a filename suffix of *.point;* this preserves the original file in case you want to create several variations.

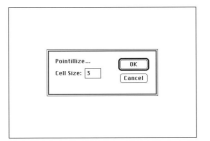

2. Choose Stylize from the Filter menu and Pointillize from the submenu. Choose a cell size between 3 and 7, depending on the effect you want. (Note also that smaller cell sizes require more memory and take longer to process.)

3. The example here was created using a cell size of 3.

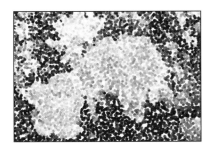

Variation: For a coarser texture, use a larger cell size. This example was created using a cell size of 7.

Variation: The Pointillize filter fills the spaces between the cells with the background color. For a different effect, change the background color. In this example, we used a light purple background and a cell size of 4.

Displace filter

1. Open the file you want to alter. Save the file with a filename suffix of *.displace;* this preserves the original file in case you want to create several variations.

2. Choose Distort from the Filter menu and Displace from the submenu. Experiment with different Displace filter options to create different effects. For this example, we used the default Horizontal and Vertical Scale values of 10 pixels and the Tile and Wraparound options.

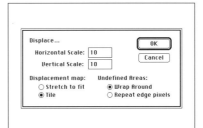

3. After you click OK, you are prompted to select a displacement map. This is the file that determines how the image is displaced. Pre-defined displacement maps can be found in the Photoshop Plug-ins and Filters folder. The example here was created using the *Random Strokes* displacement map.

4. You can use any Photoshop file as a displacement map (except bitmaps). This example was created by displacing the red and green channels using one of the custom textures from page 50 (texture #6). The green channel was then offset slightly using the Offset filter.

◟ *Selecting a background color*

To select a background color that goes well with your photograph, try using a color that already exists in the artwork. To do this, choose the eyedropper tool, hold down the Option key, and drag the eyedropper around the screen. As you do this, the background color displayed in the toolbox changes. Release the mouse button when the color is as you want it.

Stippling

Software needed: Adobe Photoshop 2.0

Use this technique to make illustrations appear as though they've been painted with a coarse coat of spray paint. To do this, you create a textured file in an extra channel using the Add Noise filter and then paint "through" the texture in the original image channel. You do this for each color in your image, so it's helpful to create masks, or selection paths, for each shape that will be a different color.

Because the effects of the Add Noise filter vary significantly at different resolutions, in many cases, this technique can't be proofed adequately on-screen. Use the chart at the end of this procedure to compare the printed results of applying different amounts of the filter to images at different resolutions.

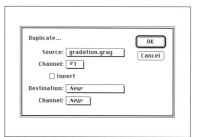

1. Open the file that you want to add texture to, and convert it to a grayscale file using the Mode menu. In most cases, you'll use this technique with blends or in shaded areas of your image.

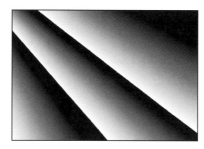

2. Select Calculate from the Image menu and Duplicate from the submenu. Duplicate the grayscale image to a new file; this will be your texture file. Duplicating is a quick way to create a file with the exact dimensions and resolution as the original file. Save the file with a suffix of *.stippled*. Keep your original grayscale file open for later use.

3. Now delete the grayscale image from your new file by choosing Select All (⌘A) and pressing Delete. You will gradually replace this image with the stippled version.

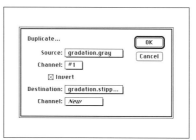

4. Convert the file to RGB mode so that you can add color. Use the Duplicate command again to copy the original grayscale file into a new channel of your stippled file. Be sure that the Invert option is selected in the Duplicate dialog box. This creates a negative of the image that you can paint through.

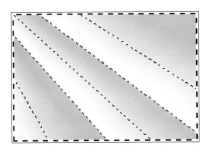

5. Return to the RGB image channel (⌘0), and choose Load Selection from the Select menu. Select Show Palette from the Window menu, and select your base color. Fill the selection with the base color (Option-Delete). This gives you a colorized version of the original grayscale image.

6. Choose New Channel from the Mode menu; then load selection #4. Apply the Add Noise filter using an Amount of 300 and the Gaussian Distribution option. Deselect (⌘D), and invert the image (⌘I).

7. Now add the first layer of texture to your image. Return to the RGB channel (⌘0), and load selection #5. Select a slightly darker new color. Hide the selection edges (⌘H) so that you can see the image clearly while you experiment with colors. Fill the selection (Option-Delete); then deselect (⌘D).

8. To create a second layer for the image, repeat step 6 using an Amount of 200 in the Add Noise filter dialog box. (Press ⌘-Option-F to open the dialog box for the last used filter.) Deselect (⌘D), and invert the image (⌘I).

9. Now add the second layer of texture to your image. Return to the RGB channel (⌘0), and load selection #6. Select a slightly darker color, and hide the selection edges to view color better (⌘H). Fill the selection (Option-Delete); then deselect (⌘D).

10. To create a third layer, repeat step 6 using an Amount of 100 in the Add Noise filter dialog box. Deselect (⌘D), and invert the image (⌘I).

11. To add the third layer of texture to your image, return to the RGB image (⌘0), load selection #7, and fill it with a third color (Option-Delete). For the last layer, black or a complementary color works well. In this example, we used a warm brown. Deselect the image (⌘D).

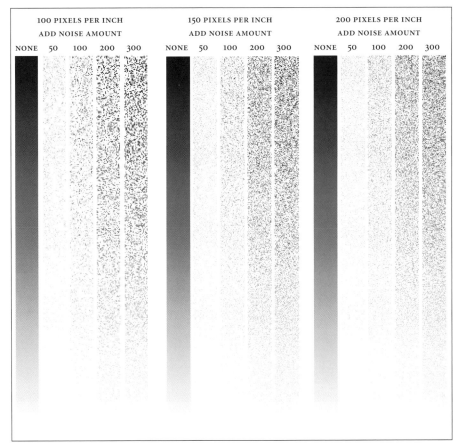

Drop shadows for objects

Software needed: Adobe Photoshop 2.0

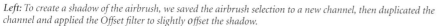

Left: *To create a shadow of the airbrush, we saved the airbrush selection to a new channel, then duplicated the channel and applied the Offset filter to slightly offset the shadow.*
Top: *Two shadows were created for this illustration: the triangular shadow was filled by blending between a lighter and darker shade of gray using the Darken Only option.*
Bottom: *For both the yo-yo and the string, the selection was saved to a new channel and then duplicated and offset. The Levels dialog box was used to darken the shadow area to retain the background pattern.*

1. Open the image in which you want a drop shadow. If you plan on separating the image, convert the image to CMYK mode. This ensures that the black you assign to the shadow is a true 100-percent black (K) and helps prevent moiré patterns in the printed artwork.

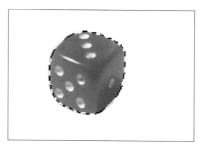

2. Select the object using a 1-point feathered edge with the lasso tool or using an anti-aliased edge with the pen tool or magic wand tool. (See the tip at the end of this procedure on combining selection tools.) Choose Save Selection from the Select menu; this saves the image in a new channel (channel #5 if you are in CMYK mode).

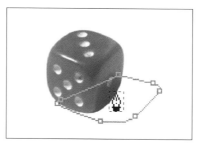

3. Return to the original image (⌘0). With the pen tool, draw the shadow area. Make sure that the shadow overlaps the image. Click inside the pen tool path to make it a selection border.

4. Choose Save Selection to save the shadow selection to a new channel (channel #6).

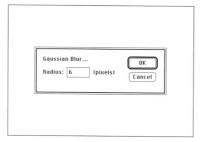

5. To soften the edges of the shadow, choose Blur from the Filter menu and Gaussian Blur from submenu. Enter a radius for the blur, and click OK.

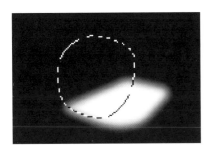

6. Choose Load Selection from the Select menu to load the selection from channel #5 into channel #6.

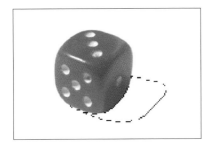

7. Make sure that the foreground color is black; then fill the selection (Option-Delete). Deselect everything (⌘D). This creates a mask for the shadow that will fit around the base of the object.

8. Return to the original image (⌘0), and load the mask from channel #6.

9. Fill the shadow with some percentage of black (we used 60%). Deselect (⌘D).

Enhancement: To clean up the edge between the shadow and the object, load selection #5, and choose Hide Edges from the Select menu (⌘H). This masks the subject to protect it while painting. Zoom in on the image where the shadow meets the object.

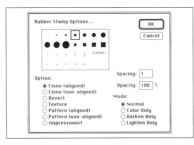

Double-click the rubber stamp tool, and select a small size brush from the dialog box. Make sure that the Clone (Aligned) option is selected, and click OK.

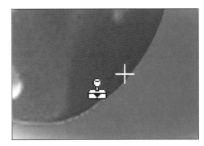

Option-click the image just above the shadow to sample the image; then clone that part of the object into the unfilled area.

When you have finished, zoom out to check the image.

❧ *Combining selection tools*

To make a complex selection, it's often best to use the magic wand tool to select large areas and the lasso tool to touch-up the selection edges. For a soft-edged selection, select the Anti-aliased option with the magic wand tool and specify a Feather radius for the lasso tool. Anti-aliasing softens the edge of the selection by assigning intermediate color values to adjacent pixels; feathering actually spreads the edge of the selection slightly using increasingly lighter color values.

As a rule of thumb, a feather radius of 1.0 for the lasso tool gives you approximately the same softening of edges as the Anti-aliased option with the magic wand tool. If you are combining selection methods and you find that the edges are still not similar enough, convert the selection to a pen tool path using the Make Path command and then click inside the path to convert it back to a selection. You can also try saving the selection to an alpha channel and using the blur tool with a very small brush size to touch up the inconsistent areas of your selection edges.

Hand-coloring photographs

Software needed: Adobe Photoshop 2.0

1. Open a grayscale Adobe Photoshop file, and convert it to RGB mode. If you are beginning with a color file, convert the file to Gray Scale mode and then back to RGB mode. Save the converted RGB file with a suffix of *.rgb* to preserve a copy of the original image.

2. Select a large area of the image to be colored (for example, the background). If you are selecting with the pen or magic wand tool, turn on the Anti-aliased option; if you are selecting with the the lasso tool, use a Feather radius of 1. In this example, we selected the area using the magic wand and then the lasso tool.

3. When the selection is as you want it, choose Save Selection from the Select menu. This preserves the selection in case you want to reuse it.

4. Return to the RGB channel (⌘0), choose Load Selection to load the selection back into the channel, and hide the selection edges (⌘H).

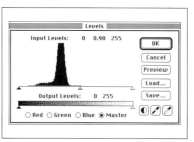

5. If the photograph is light, open the Levels dialog box under the Image menu (⌘L), and drag the gray midtone (gamma) triangle to the right just slightly to bring up the black. This extra black helps preserve detail after color has been added. Click OK.

6. Now use the Color Balance dialog box under the Image menu (⌘Y) to add color to the image. Adjust the shadows, midtones, and highlights, using the Preview button to check the results. When the color is as you want it, click OK.

7. To color small areas of the image, repeat steps 2-5. (Alternatively, you can paint without making any selections for a more freehand look.)

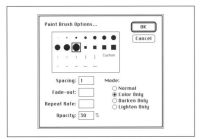

8. Select the color you want to paint with; then double-click the paint brush in the toolbox, and select a brush size. Start with an opacity of 30%, and select the Color Only option. The Color Only option lets you replace the color of the pixels while retaining the gray levels.

9. Paint the area. If you are not satisfied with the effect, choose Undo from the Edit menu (⌘Z), and change the opacity. (See the tip at the end of this procedure.) Note that to apply a second coat of color to an area, you must release the mouse button between strokes.

Variation: To make a sepia-tone photograph, follow step 1; then choose Color Balance from the Image menu and adjust the shadows, midtones, and highlights as follows:

	R	G	B
Shadows	+23	+5	-15
Midtones	+25	0	-14
Highlights	+19	0	-15

◠ *Changing the paint opacity*

When using a drawing tool, such as the paint brush, you can change the opacity of the paint by typing a number from 1 (10% opacity) to 9 (90% opacity) on the keyboard. Typing 0 changes the opacity to 100%.

◠ *Using the Levels dialog box*

When using the Levels dialog box, you can preview the tonal compression while you make adjustments. To do this, simply hold down the Option key as you adjust the Input Levels controls: a high-contrast preview appears, indicating the areas of the image being altered. This feature is also useful when adjusting the individual color components of an image using the radio buttons at the bottom of the Levels dialog box. In this case, the black in the high-contrast preview indicates where none of the given color component exists.

Original image

High-contrast preview: red channel

Also, a little-known trick for comparing an image before and after an adjustment is to click the title bar at the top of the dialog box. This feature works in all the color correction dialog boxes.

Linear spectrums

Software needed: Adobe Illustrator 3

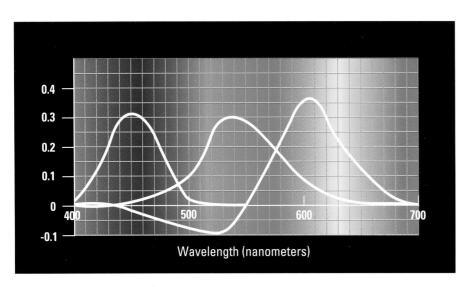

0.4
0.3
0.2
0.1
0
-0.1

400   500   600   700

Wavelength (nanometers)

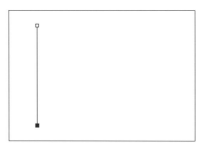

1. Open the file in which you want to create a spectrum. Select the pen tool, and click once to define an endpoint; then hold down the Shift key to constrain the angle, and click again to define the other endpoint. Position the line where you want the spectrum to begin, leaving space for five additional lines to define the spectrum.

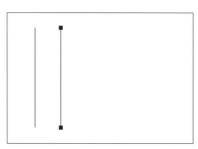

2. Select the line, and Option-click the selection tool in the toolbox to open the Move dialog box. Enter a Horizontal value, and click Copy.

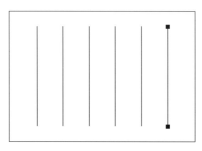

3. Choose the Transform Again command (⌘D) four times to create four additional lines. Each line will define a color in the spectrum.

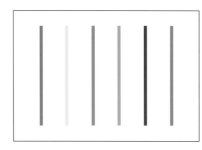

4. Paint each line with a 2.5-point stroke using the following colors (from left to right):

Red:	100% M	Cyan:	100% C
	100% Y	Violet:	100% C
Yellow:	100% Y		100% M
Green:	100% C	Magenta:	100% M
	100% Y		

Preview (⌘Y) to check your work.

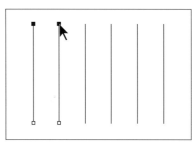

5. Now you will create blends between each pair of adjacent lines, from left to right. Select an endpoint of the first line with the selection tool; then hold down the Shift key, and select the same endpoint of the next line.

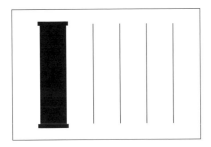

6. With the two lines selected, choose the blend tool, and click the endpoint of each line. Click OK in the Blend dialog box to accept the recommended number of steps; this number is based on the percent of color change between the two lines. (See pages 38-41 for more information on blends.)

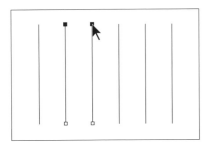

7. Hide the blend (⌘3); then choose the selection tool, and select the top points of the second and third lines.

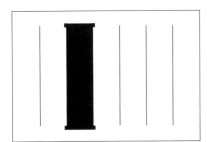

8. Create the blend as you did in step 6, using Illustrator's recommended number of steps; then hide the blend (⌘3).

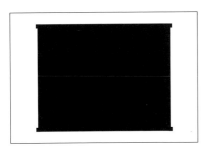

9. Continue creating and hiding blends until you have blended all the lines; then select Show All (⌘4) to reveal the blends.

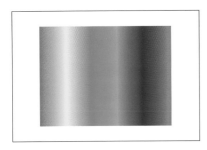

10. Preview the results (⌘Y).

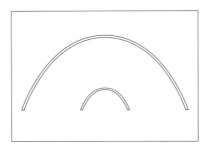

Variation: You can create a variety of different-shaped spectrums using this technique. To create a rainbow, begin by drawing two arcs: one for the inside of the blend and one for the outside. Use filled shapes for curved blends instead of stroked lines. (See page 40.)

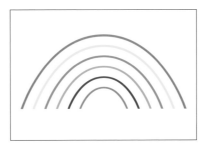

Option-select both arcs, choose the blend tool, and click the bottom right corner point of each arc. Specify 4 steps for the blend, and click OK. This gives you a total of six evenly spaced and scaled arcs.

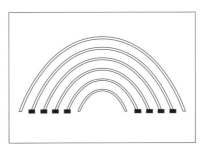

Select the four middle arcs, and ungroup them (⌘U). Paint each of the six arcs with the colors from step 4.

Blend the arcs together as described in steps 5-10. Be sure that you click corresponding points of each arc to create the blend.

Full-color spectrums

Software needed: Adobe Photoshop 2.0

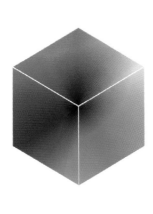

A color spectrum in Adobe Photoshop is achieved by making a blend from the foreground color to the background color. You can blend the colors using the CMYK/RGB color space option, which creates a blend through the intermediate gray levels between the colors, or you can blend the colors using the HSB (Hue, Saturation, and Brightness) color space option, which creates a blend through the hues displayed on a color wheel. This second option lets you create a full-color spectrum by specifying two almost identical colors so that all the hues on the color wheel appear in the blend.

Top Left: *An HSB-CW blend from green to red. Typeface: Ryumin™ Light-KL.*
Top Right: *We created a linear spectrum and applied the Polar Coordinates filter; we then masked the spectrum using a cube created in Illustrator. In HSB mode, we created a blend from black to white in the Brightness channel using the RGB/CMYK and Radial options, an opacity of 80%, and a midpoint skew of 40.*
Bottom Left: *An HSB-CW blend from red to purple was pasted into the image and feathered. The Paste Controls dialog box was used to lighten the rainbow. Distort, Skew, and Perspective were used to position the rainbow.*

Creating a linear spectrum
1. Open a new RGB file.

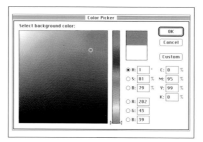

2. Choose a foreground and background color. These colors will be the beginning and ending colors of your blend, respectively. To create a full spectrum as in this example, specify a red foreground color of 96% M and 99% Y and a red background color of 95% M and 99% Y.

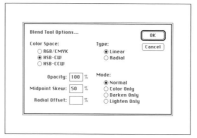

3. Double-click the blend tool to open the Blend dialog box. Select the HSB-CW (clockwise) and Linear options, and click OK. You can also change the midpoint skew to move the midpoint of your blend. This condenses one side of the blend and expands the other.

4. With the blend tool still selected, click and drag from left to right to define the line along which the blend is created (hold down the Shift key to constrain the line horizontally). If the line is shorter than the image area, the area on the left and right of the line is filled with the starting and ending colors, respectively.

Creating a circular spectrum

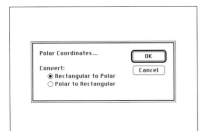

1. Follow steps 1-4 to create a linear spectrum. Choose Distort from the Filter menu and Polar Coordinates from the submenu. Select the Rectangular to Polar option to change from rectangular to polar coordinates, and click OK.

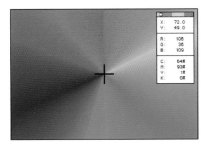

2. Choose Show Info from the Window menu. Select the elliptical marquee tool, position the pointer in the center of the spectrum, and note the *x, y* coordinates in the Show Info window.

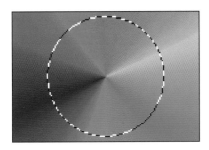

3. With the pointer still positioned on the *x, y* coordinates, hold down the Option and Shift keys to draw the marquee from its center and constrain it to a circle, and drag outward. When the circle is the size you want, release the mouse button and then the Option and Shift keys.

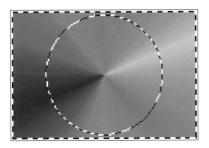

4. Choose Inverse from the Select menu to invert the selection. This selects everything outside the circle.

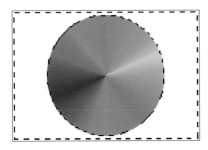

5. To fill the selection with white, double-click the eyedropper tool to make the foreground and background colors black and white, respectively; then press Delete to fill the selection with the background color.

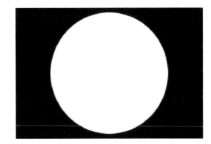

Enhancement: You can create a blend in the saturation channel of the image to soften the effect of the spectrum. To do this, make sure that the background is still selected; then choose Save Selection from the Select menu. Invert the new channel (⌘I).

Use the Mode menu to convert the image to HSB Color mode. Go to the Saturation channel (⌘2); this is where you will create the radial blend. Double-click the eyedropper tool to make the foreground and background colors black and white, respectively. In the saturation channel, black represents 0% saturation and white represents 100% saturation.

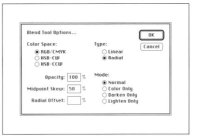

Double-click the blend tool to open the Blend dialog box. Choose the RGB/CMYK Color Space option and the Radial Type option. Click OK.

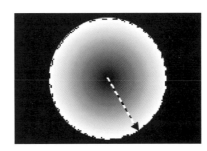

Choose Load Selection from the Select menu. With the blend tool selected, position the pointer at the coordinates you recorded in step 2. Holding down the Shift key to constrain the angle of the line, drag to the outside of the circle.

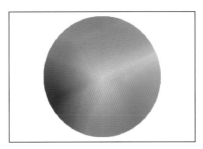

Deselect the circle (⌘D), and reconvert the image to RGB Color mode. The colors in the spectrum are blended from 0% saturation at the center to 100% at the outer edge.

Generating smooth blends

Software needed: Adobe Illustrator 3, Adobe Photoshop 2.0

Shade-stepping, or banding, in printed gradations is caused by a limitation in the number of gray levels an imagesetter can create. The maximum number of gray levels an imagesetter can create is 256. Whether or not this presents a problem for your artwork depends on the length of your blend, the colors in the blend, and — in Adobe Illustrator — the number of steps you specify. This section explains the factors involved in blending and provides guidelines for creating blends without banding. It also describes how to use the Add Noise filter to compensate for potential banding problems.

The best way to ensure that your blends print without banding is to figure out all the variables involved in printing the blend and then compensate where possible in how you create the blend. The factors that affect how a blend prints include:

- The resolution and line screen combination.
- The percent of change from the beginning to the end of your blend. Less than a 50% change can cause banding.
- The length of your blend. The length you can use varies with the colors in your blend, but as a general rule, the blend length shouldn't exceed 7.5 inches.
- The colors you use. Blends between very dark colors and white seem to generate the most banding problems. If possible, use lighter colors or make dark blends short; avoid very dark colors in blends larger than 7.5 inches.

Determining the best resolution/line screen combination

With most printers, increasing the screen frequency decreases the number of gray levels available to the printer. If the number of gray levels is less than the number required for your blend, the result is a posterized gradation. Before you create your artwork, find out what resolution and line screen will be used to print the artwork. These two numbers determine the number of gray levels the imagesetter can print. If you know the line screen but the resolution hasn't yet been decided, use the table shown here to determine the minimum resolution needed to print that line screen. For example, if you are creating artwork for a publication that always prints at a line screen of 150, you need to print film at a resolution of 2400 or more to get 256 levels of gray. If you print at a lower resolution, you won't get 256 levels of gray, and you may see banding in your blends. If you can't adjust the line screen or resolution to get 256 grays, find out what these values are, and follow the guidelines described under "Using Formulas for Special Cases," on page 40.

FINAL IMAGESETTER RESOLUTION	MAXIMUM LINE SCREEN TO USE
300	19
400	25
600	38
900	56
1000	63
1270	79
1446	90
1524	95
1693	106
2000	125
2400	150
2540	159
3000	188
3252	203
3600	225
4000	250

100%   100%   100%   100%

5″

0%   20%   50%   75%

Keep the percent change larger than 50% – These 5″ black gradations were printed at 2540 dpi with a 150 line screen. While the two on the left contain enough steps to avoid banding, the two on the right do not.

Use the correct combination of resolution and screen frequency – Refer to the table on the left to find the correct resolution to use with your line screen. The three blends shown on the left contain banding caused by the wrong resolution/line screen combination.

**1270 DPI
150 LINE SCREEN**

**2540 DPI
150 LINE SCREEN**

Determining the maximum blend length in Adobe Illustrator

Adobe Illustrator calculates the number of steps required for each blend based on the percent change between the colors in the blend. The number of steps in the blend determines the maximum length the blend can be without generating banding. Use this procedure to determine whether your blend is too long. Note that Illustrator's recommended number of steps are based on the assumption that the blend will be printed with a line screen and resolution combination that provides 256 levels of gray. If this is not the case, see "Using Formulas for Special Cases."

1. Create the beginning and ending shapes of your blend. See page 40 to determine whether you should use shapes or lines. Select the measure tool, and click the top leftmost point of the two lines or shapes; then click the corresponding point of the right line or shape.

2. Write down the distance displayed in the Measure dialog box. The distance will be displayed in inches, points, or centimeters, depending on the Ruler Units specified in the Preferences dialog box (⌘K). This distance represents the length of your blend. Click OK.

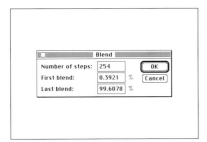

3. Make sure that both blend shapes are selected. Choose the blend tool from the toolbox, and click on corresponding points of the shapes. Adobe Illustrator calculates the number of steps needed for the blend based on the percentages of color in the first and last step.

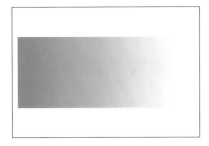

4. Now look at the table on this page. Using the number of steps calculated in step 3, see if the length that you wrote down in step 2 is greater than the maximum length indicated in the chart. If it isn't, click OK to create the blend. If it is, reduce the length of the blend, change the colors, or use the Add Noise filter to smooth the blend using the procedure described on page 41.

NUMBER OF STEPS ADOBE ILLUSTRATOR RECOMMENDS	MAXIMUM BLEND LENGTH		
	POINTS	INCHES	CMS
10	21.6	.3	.762
20	43.2	.6	1.524
30	64.8	.9	2.286
40	86.4	1.2	3.048
50	108.0	1.5	3.810
60	129.6	1.8	4.572
70	151.2	2.1	5.334
80	172.8	2.4	6.096
90	194.4	2.7	6.858
100	216.0	3.0	7.620
110	237.6	3.3	8.382
120	259.2	3.6	9.144
130	280.8	3.9	9.906
140	302.4	4.2	10.668
150	324.0	4.5	11.430
160	345.6	4.8	12.192
170	367.2	5.1	12.954
180	388.8	5.4	13.716
190	410.4	5.7	14.478
200	432.0	6.0	15.240
210	453.6	6.3	16.002
220	475.2	6.6	16.764
230	496.8	6.9	17.526
240	518.4	7.2	18.288
250	540.0	7.5	19.050
256	553.0	7.7	19.507

Will I get shade-stepping with my blend? – *If you know the length of your blend and the number of steps available, you can use this table to determine whether you will get banding in your blend. If your blend length exceeds the maximum length shown here for the number of steps available, you may get banding. Remember that Illustrator determines the number of steps available based on the assumption that the resolution and line screen provide 256 grays (see the table on page 38).*

Evaluating film before it goes to press

While creating color proofs before going to press is always recommended, it's especially important if your artwork contains blends. In some cases, banding that appears on film disappears on the press. For example, banding in the 0% to 5% area or the 95% to 100% area of a blend usually disappears on press, since printing presses typically can't hold a dot this small. Banding in the midtone region of a blend, however, may appear on press. To correct this problem, you can try remaking the blend using the guidelines in this section or try smoothing the blend using the Add Noise filter (see page 41). If a project is very critical or expensive, you may want to run a press proof to check for banding and other printing problems.

Blending between lines versus shapes in Adobe Illustrator

One way to save disk space and imaging time when creating linear blends is to use lines with thick strokes instead of rectangles. This works because a stroke consists of two points while a box is made up of four (the blend tool leaves out the center point). If your file contains large blends or very many blends, those extra points can result in a file size 1½ to 2 times the size of a file containing the same blends using lines. Depending on your network, it may also take more than 1.5 times as long to print the file. Note, however, that the savings in imaging time occurs only with linear gradations. Using curved strokes can result in extra imaging time as well as cause fitting problems in corners areas. For odd-shaped gradations, closed paths give better results than stroked lines.

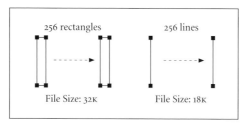

File Size: 32K   File Size: 18K

Using stroked lines instead of rectangles to create linear blends can significantly decrease your file size.

If you do use strokes in your blends, make sure that the line weight is thick enough to overlap the adjacent line. You can double-check this by zooming in on the blend and previewing it to make sure no gap exists, or you can calculate the minimum line weight by dividing the length of your blend in points by the number of steps Adobe Illustrator recommends.

Finally, remember that lines are stroked from the center out. This means that the outside edges of the blend will extend half the stroke weight in length past the lines as displayed in Artwork Only mode. You may need to adjust the outside edges of the gradation to compensate for this.

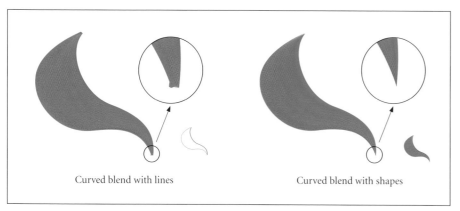

Curved blend with lines   Curved blend with shapes

For creating curved blends, shapes often give better results than lines, generating more precise points at the tips of the curves.

Using formulas for special cases

If you've found that the resolution/line screen combination you are using to print your artwork does not give you 256 grays, you still might be able to avoid banding by changing the number of steps in the Blend dialog box. Below are some formulas you can use to calculate the precise number of steps that you need in this situation.

If you're creating a blend in Adobe Photoshop, you won't be able to adjust the number of steps; however, you can use these formulas to figure out whether or not you can expect to see banding in your blend. If the step length calculated in step 4 is greater than 2.16 points (0.3 inches), you may get some banding.

1. Calculate the number of grays available for your output using the following formula:

$$\text{Number of grays} = \{\text{Resolution (dpi)} \div \text{Line screen (lpi)}\}^2$$

2. Calculate the number of steps available for your blend using the following formula:

$$\text{Number of steps} = \text{Number of grays} \times \text{Percent change in color}$$

To figure out the percent change in color, subtract the lower value from the higher value (for example, a blend between 50% black and 100% black indicates a 50% change in color.) When blending process color combinations, identify the largest percent change between process colors. For example, a blend from 10% yellow and 50% magenta to 80% yellow and 70% magenta indicates a 70% change, dictated by the change in yellow.

3. If you are creating your blend in Adobe Illustrator, enter the number of steps from step 2 in the Blend dialog box. Entering fewer steps than this will give you fewer gray levels than are available, and so may cause banding; entering more steps will increase the file size with no improvement in the printed output.

4. Now calculate the length of each step in the blend. If the step length is 2.16 points (.03 inches) or less, you should not get banding in the final output. If the length is greater than 2.16 points, you may get banding, depending on the colors used in the blend. In this case, decrease the length of the blend or use the Add Noise filter in Adobe Photoshop to smooth the blend as described in the following procedure.

$$\text{Step length} = \text{Blend length} \div \text{Steps available}$$

Adding noise to smooth out gradation banding

You can also use the Adobe Photoshop Add Noise filter to compensate for banding in gradations. The Add Noise filter compensates for banding in two ways. First, it tricks the eye into seeing more shades of gray than the printer can produce by randomly scattering the available shades into a pattern, creating a dithering effect. Second, the Add Noise filter covers up flaws and streaks by adding pixels. To ensure that the filter doesn't create new color values in the image, it's important to apply the filter to each channel individually.

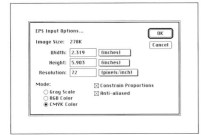

1. Open your Adobe Illustrator file in Adobe Photoshop (Photoshop automatically opens color Illustrator files in CMYK mode), or if you have created your gradation in Photoshop, convert the RGB image to CMYK mode by choosing CMYK from the Mode menu.

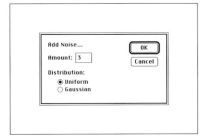

2. Use the keyboard shortcuts to open each of the individual color channels (⌘-1, 2, 3, and 4), and apply the Add Noise filter to each channel that displays an image. *Do not apply the filter to a channel if it contains no visible image.* The shortcut for reusing a filter is ⌘F. Refer to the sample blends on the right to determine the amount of noise needed for your blend.

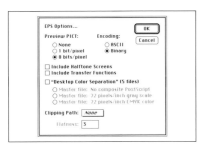

3. To use this file in other documents, save the file in EPS format. Be sure to save it using the Binary format option; a file saved in binary format prints twice as fast as the same file saved in ASCII format. Note that PageMaker® and FrameMaker® are not compatible with files saved in the Binary format, so you must save files for these programs in ASCII format.

Use these examples to help you determine the amount of noise needed to smooth out your blend. Notice that in the examples created using large amounts of noise, the white areas of the blends take on a subtle tone of color.

| 0 | 3 | 5 | 7 | 10 |

AMOUNT OF NOISE ADDED

4 Patterns and Textures

Constructing simple patterns

Software needed: Adobe Illustrator 3

The simplest way to construct a pattern tile is to draw any graphic object and surround it with a rectangle placed in the background. The following procedure describes how to create denser patterns that tile perfectly by positioning copies of the graphic object you are using in each of the corners of the pattern rectangle. Once you've created a pattern, you can use it in your artwork and embed it in other documents; you can then alter the pattern in the artwork without changing the original design.

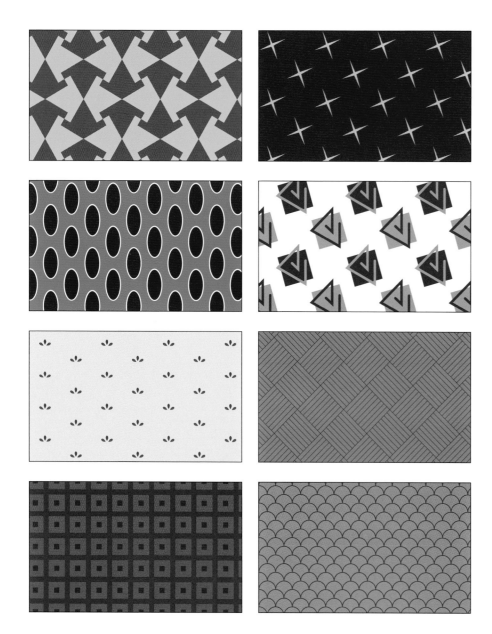

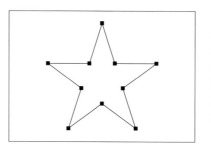

1. Select the artwork that you want to use as a repeating element in your pattern. (Remember that a pattern may not contain EPS images, masked groups, or elements painted with other patterns.) Group the selection (⌘G). In the Preferences dialog box (⌘K), turn on the Snap to Point option.

2. In the Paint dialog box (⌘I), specify the paint attributes you want for the object. Do not paint the object with a pattern. Preview (⌘Y) to check the results.

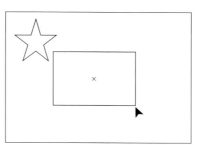

3. Draw a rectangle the size you want the pattern tile to be. For the best results, the rectangle should be about one square inch. If necessary, you can start with a larger rectangle and then scale it down in step 10. Note that the rectangle must have square corners — that is, if you use the rectangle tool, the corner radius must be 0.

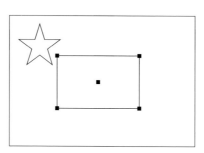

4. The paint attributes of the rectangle define your pattern's background. Fill and stroke the rectangle with None for a transparent background, or paint it for a solid background. If you want your tile boundaries to be outlined in the final pattern, stroke the rectangle. Send the rectangle to the back (⌘-).

5. Position the object over the left corner of the rectangle. Preview (⌘Y) to check your work.

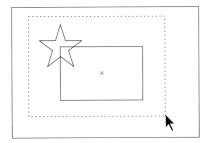

6. Select both the rectangle and the object.

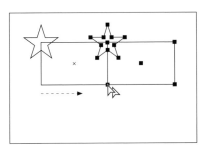

7. Place the pointer on the lower left corner of the rectangle, and begin dragging the artwork to the right; then hold down the Option and Shift keys to create a copy and to constrain its movement horizontally. When the left corner of the new rectangle "snaps to" the right corner of the original, release the mouse button and then the Option and Shift keys.

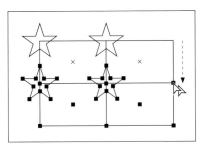

8. Select all of the pattern artwork. Begin dragging the artwork downward by one of the upper corner points; then hold down the Option and Shift keys to create a copy and to constrain its movement. When the upper corner of the copy "snaps to" the lower corner of the original, release the mouse button and then the Option and Shift keys.

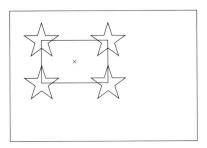

9. Delete all rectangles but the first (in this case, the upper left rectangle). The remaining rectangle defines the boundaries of the pattern tile.

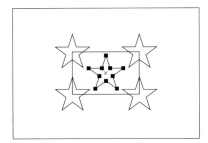

10. Place any additional graphics you want within the rectangle. Be sure these elements don't overlap the bounding rectangle, or the pattern won't tile correctly. If you began with a rectangle larger than one square inch, scale the artwork for more efficient tiling.

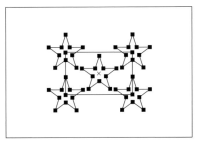

11. Preview the pattern tile (⌘Y). If you plan to experiment with different colors or to transform the pattern tile, group all of the elements (⌘G).

12. Select the rectangle and its contents.

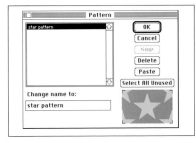

13. Open the Pattern dialog box under the Paint menu, and click New. A preview of the new pattern tile appears in the lower right corner of the dialog box. You can now name the pattern. Click OK; the new pattern is now embedded in your artwork.

14. Create a shape, fill it with your new pattern (⌘I), and preview the results (⌘Y).

Constructing polygons
for patterns

Software needed: Adobe Illustrator 3

To construct a geometric pattern that tiles uniformly, it's important to begin with a perfect geometric shape, or polygon. To do this, you first define the center point and one of the corner points of the polygon. You then use the rotate tool to precisely define the remaining corner points of the polygon. The angle of rotation for each corner point is defined by dividing 360 degrees by the number of sides of the polygon; the correct values are provided in the following chart.

SHAPE	NUMBER OF SIDES	ROTATION ANGLE	SHAPE	NUMBER OF SIDES	ROTATION ANGLE
△	3	120°	⬡	7	51.4285°
▢	4	90°	⬡	8	45°
⬠	5	72°	⬡	9	40°
⬡	6	60°	⬡	10	36°

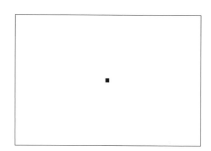

1. In the Preferences dialog box (⌘K), set the Ruler Units to Picas/Points, and turn on the Snap to Point option. Select the pen tool, and click once to set the center point of your polygon.

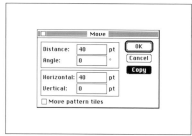

2. Hold down the Option key, and click the selection tool in the toolbox to open the Move dialog box. Enter the distance you want between the center point and the first corner point of the polygon (we used 40 points), and click Copy. This sets the first corner point of the polygon.

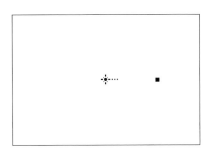

3. To create the next corner point, make sure that the first corner point is selected; then select the rotate tool, and Option-click the center point you set in step 1.

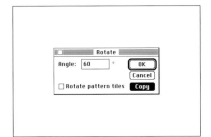

4. Enter the appropriate angle for your polygon in the Rotate dialog box (see the chart at the beginning of this procedure); then click Copy.

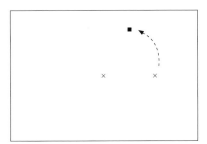

5. To create each of the remaining corner points, select Transform Again from the Arrange menu (⌘D). Create one point for each corner of the polygon. Be sure to select Transform Again only once for each point.

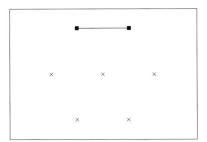

6. To join the sides of the polygon, use the selection tool to click any corner point of the polygon; then Shift-click an adjacent point, and select Join from the Arrange menu (⌘J). Deselect the first corner point, and continue Shift-clicking and selecting Join until the polygon is a closed path.

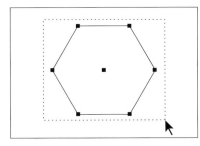

7. Use the marquee to select the polygon and its center point; then group them (⌘G).

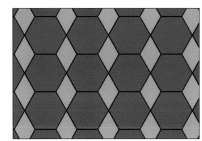

8. Construct the pattern using the procedure described in the previous technique, "Constructing Simple Patterns." The result is a perfect geometric pattern.

❧ *Creating a 5-pointed star*

Using the procedure described above, create a 10-sided polygon. Use the direct-selection tool to select 5 of the points so that every second point is selected.

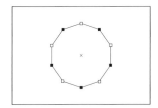

Choose the scale tool from the toolbox. Position the cursor over the center point of the polygon, hold down the Option key, and click. Type 50% in the dialog box, and click OK.

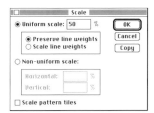

Paint the star (⌘I), and preview (⌘Y) to check your work.

Using patterns to create textures

Software needed: Adobe Illustrator 3

You can create the effect of an uneven texture by constructing a pattern that appears irregular when it tiles. To achieve this effect, the edges of the pattern tile must match up perfectly so that the tiling results in one continuous texture.

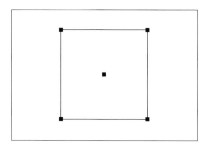

1. Make sure that the Snap to Point option is turned on in the Preferences dialog box (⌘K). Use the rectangle tool to draw the bounding rectangle for your pattern tile. For efficient printing, the finished tile should be approximately one square inch; if you wish, you can start with a larger rectangle and scale it later (step 10).

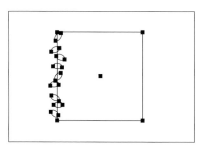

2. Begin drawing your texture with shapes or lines that intersect only the left side of the bounding rectangle. When you have finished, select the rectangle and the texture.

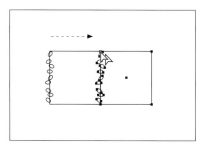

3. Place the pointer on the upper left corner of the rectangle. Begin dragging the artwork to the right; then press the Option and Shift keys to make a copy and to constrain its movement horizontally. When the upper left corner of the copy "snaps to" the upper right corner of the original, release the mouse button and then the Option and Shift keys.

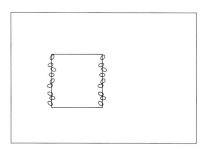

4. Select the right rectangle and delete it.

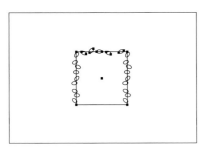

5. Continue drawing your texture with shapes or lines that intersect only the top of the rectangle. When you have finished, select the rectangle and the top texture.

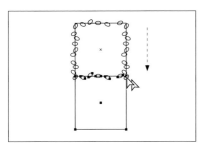

6. Place the pointer on one of the upper corner points of the rectangle. Begin dragging the selected artwork downward; then press the Option and Shift keys to make a copy and constrain its movement. When the upper corner of the copy "snaps to" the lower corner of the original, release the mouse button and then the Option and Shift keys.

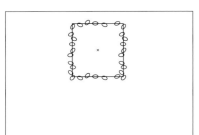

7. Select the lower rectangle, and delete it.

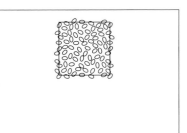

8. Fill in the middle of the rectangle with your texture. Be careful not to intersect any of the rectangle's edges.

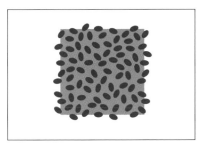

9. Select the tile artwork excluding the rectangle. Paint the texture using the Paint Style dialog box (⌘I). Next, select only the rectangle. Fill the rectangle (⌘I) — for a transparent tile background, use a fill and stroke value of None. Send the rectangle to the back (⌘-); then preview the artwork (⌘Y) to check the colors.

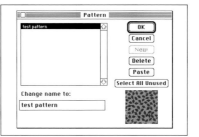

10. Select the pattern tile. If you began with a rectangle larger than one square inch, scale the artwork for more efficient tiling. With the tile still selected, open the Pattern dialog box under the Paint menu, and click New. A preview of the pattern tile appears in the lower right corner of the dialog box. Name your new pattern, and click OK.

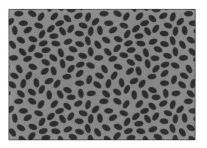

11. You are now ready to test your pattern tile. Create a shape, open the Paint Style dialog box (⌘I), and fill the shape with your new pattern. Preview the results (⌘Y).

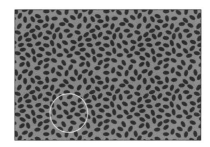

12. Now use the zoom-out tool to reduce your view of the artwork, and look for any obvious flaws in the pattern. Look for places in your textured area that create an obvious repeating pattern. If possible, print your pattern tile and mark the areas that need work.

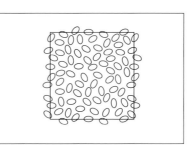

13. Return to your pattern tile, and adjust the artwork to correct the problem areas. Note that if you adjust any artwork that intersects the edges of the tile, you will need to repeat steps 3 and 6. Continue adjusting your pattern tile and previewing the textured area until no repeating patterns are obvious.

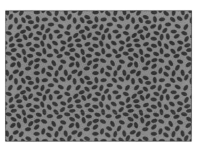

14. When you are satisfied with the tile, redefine the pattern in the Pattern dialog box, and click OK. Fill your shape again with the pattern, and preview the results (⌘Y).

Custom textures

Software needed: Adobe Photoshop 2.0

To add texture to a Adobe Photoshop image, you can define a texture as a pattern and paint with it, or create a "texture mask" in an alpha channel and paint through the mask. Most of the color samples shown here were created by filling the background with a color, loading the texture from an alpha channel, and then filling the texture with a second color.

While all the examples shown here were created at a resolution of 200 pixels per inch, different image resolutions will produce different results. At lower resolutions, the textures will appear coarser; at higher resoutions, they will be more subtle. If you are working with textures at different resolutions, be sure to proof the results on the output device you will use for the final printed piece.

GRAY SCALE   COLOR

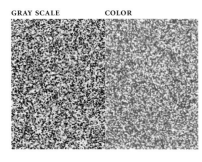

Texture 1:
New Channel or New File at 200 ppi
Pointillize filter: 3 cell size
Adjust Levels (⌘L) until input reads 212, 0.26, 255
Add Noise filter: 32, Gaussian
Equalize (⌘E)
Add Noise filter: 32, Gaussian

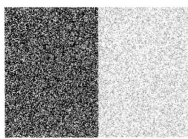

Texture 2:
New Channel or New File at 200 ppi
Select All (⌘A)
Fill with 100% Black
Add Noise filter: 300, Gaussian

Texture 3:
New Channel or New File at 200 ppi
Add Noise filter three times: 300, Gaussian

Texture 4:
New Channel or New File at 200 ppi
Add Noise filter three times: 300, Gaussian
Displace filter: 10 Horizontal and Vertical Scale,
    Stretch to fit, Wrap Around, *Random Strokes*
    displacement map

GRAY SCALE   COLOR

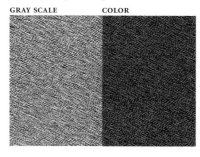

Texture 5:
New Channel or New File at 200 ppi
Add Noise filter three times: 300, Gaussian
Motion Blur filter: 21°, 10 pixels
Sharpen filter four times

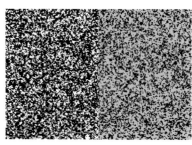

Texture 6:
New Channel or New File at 200 ppi
Add Noise filter: 300, Uniform
Ripple filter: 200, Small
Posterize: 2 Levels
Diffuse: Darken Only
Invert (⌘I)

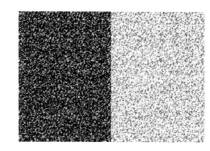

Texture 7:
Open *Intricate Surface* pattern: 72 ppi (Patterns folder)
Select All (⌘A) and Define Pattern
New Channel or New File at 200 ppi
Select All (⌘A)
Fill with 100% Pattern
Diffuse filter: Normal
Invert (⌘I)

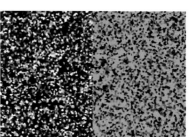

Texture 8:
New Channel or New File at 200 ppi
Select All (⌘A)
Fill with 100% Black
Add Noise filter: 300, Uniform
Crystallize: 5 Cell Size

GRAY SCALE   COLOR

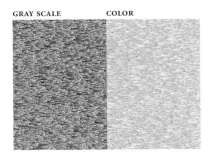

Texture 9:
New Channel or New File at 200 ppi
Select All (⌘A)
Fill with 50% Black
Add Noise filter: 5, Gaussian
Adjust Levels (⌘L): click Auto button
Wind filter three times: Stagger, Right

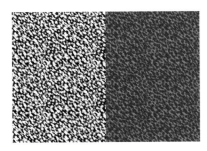

Texture 10:
Open *Mezzotint dot* pattern: 72 ppi (Patterns folder)
Select All (⌘A) and Define Pattern
New Channel or New File at 200 ppi
Select All (⌘A)
Fill with 100% Pattern
Motion Blur filter: -45° Angle, 3 Pixel Distance
Invert (⌘I)
Sharpen filter

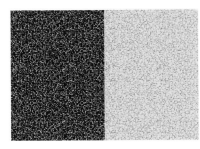

Texture 11:
Open *Mezzotint dot* pattern: 72 ppi (Patterns folder)
Select All (⌘A) and Define Pattern
New Channel or New File at 200 ppi
Select All (⌘A)
Fill with 100% Pattern
Solarize filter
Adjust Levels (⌘L): click Auto button

Texture 12:
New Channel or New File at 200 ppi
Select All (⌘A)
Fill with 25% Black
Add Noise filter: 100, Gaussian
Emboss filter: 30° Angle, 3 Height, 100%

Texture 13:
New Channel or New File at 200 ppi
Select All (⌘A)
Fill with 25% Black
Add Noise filter: 100, Gaussian
Emboss filter: 30° Angle, 3 Height, 100%
Motion Blur filter: 30° Angle, 10 Pixel Distance

GRAY SCALE   COLOR

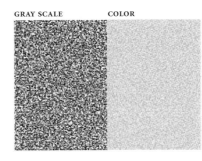

Texture 14:
New Channel or New File at 200 ppi
Select All (⌘A)
Fill with 100% Black
Add Noise filter: 50, Uniform
Pointillize filter twice: 3 Cell Size

Texture 15:
Open *Random V's* pattern: 72 ppi (Patterns folder)
Select it and Define Pattern
New Channel or New File at 200 ppi
Fill with 100% pattern
Ripple filter: 200, small

Texture 16:
Open *Herringbone* 2 pattern: 72 ppi (Patterns folder)
Select it and Define Pattern
New Channel or New File at 200 ppi
Diffuse filter three times: Lighten Only
Add Noise filter: 100, Gaussian

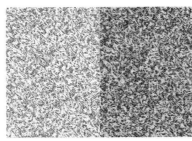

Texture 17:
Open *Mezzotint dot* pattern: 100 ppi (Patterns folder)
Select it and Define Pattern
New Channel or New File at 200 ppi
Select All (⌘A)
Fill with 50% Pattern
Ripple filter: 200, Large
Add Noise filter: 100, Uniform

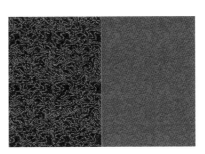

Texture 18:
Open *Wrinkle* pattern: 100 ppi (Patterns folder)
Select it and Define Pattern
New Channel or New File at 200 ppi
Select All (⌘A)
Fill with 50% Pattern and Invert (⌘I)
Diffuse filter: Lighten Only
Sharpen filter
Add Noise filter: 50, Uniform

Embellishing three-dimensional charts

Software needed: Adobe Photoshop 2.0, Adobe Illustrator 3, Adobe Type Manager, and Type 1 Fonts

1991 **Marble Sales**
In Tons

Pernice 5,000	Bianco 800	Salome 2,000	Bloodstone 2,500	Castagna 3,000

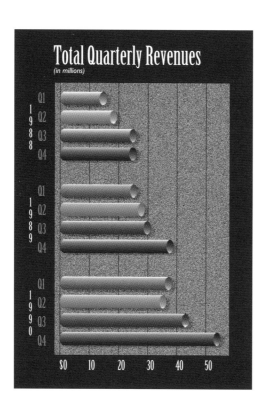

Left: This three-dimensional pie chart was created in Adobe Illustrator and then embellished in Adobe Photoshop with photographs of different kinds of marble. Typeface: Walbaum™ OsF.
Right: This bar chart was created in Illustrator and then opened in Photoshop where the blends were added. The background was created using the Add Noise filter and then pasted behind the chart. Typefaces: Birch and Gill Sans® Condensed.

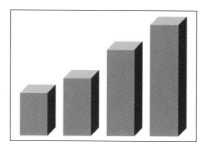

1. Create a three-dimensional chart in Adobe Illustrator using one of the procedures described in Section 2. Remove all type and extra lines from the chart, and save the file. Open the file in Adobe Photoshop as an RGB document at the size you want and at a resolution of one and one-half to two times the line screen you will use to print.

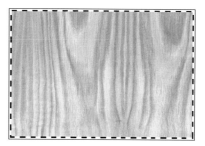

2. Open a Photoshop file with a texture or an image that you want to appear in your chart. Make sure that the file's resolution is the same as your chart. (If necessary, use the Image Size command to change the resolution of the image.) Select the texture or image, and copy it to the Clipboard (⌘C).

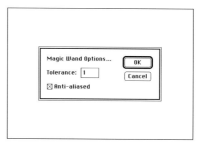

3. Double-click the magic wand tool, and set the Tolerance value to 1. This causes the magic wand tool to select only pixels with exactly the same color value as the pixel you click.

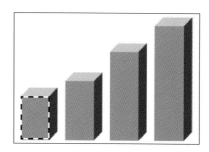

4. Click inside one of the front surfaces of the pie or bar chart to select the surface. (If you plan to make identical adjustments to all surfaces of the same color, choose Similar from the Select menu.)

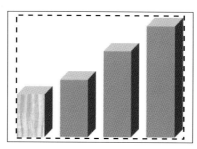

5. Choose Paste Into from the Edit menu to copy the image from the Clipboard into the selected surface. If you wish to reposition the image, use the selection tool to move the image around within the surface.

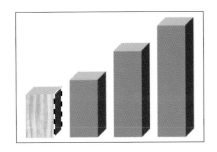

6. Deselect the artwork (⌘D). With the magic wand tool, click the corresponding side section of the surface you have just modified. (Note that this procedure may vary slightly depending on the type of chart you are using.)

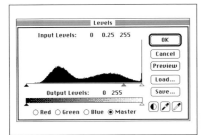

7. Choose Paste Into from the Edit menu.

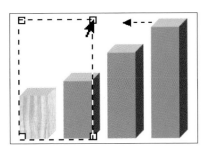

8. Open the Levels dialog box under the Image menu (⌘L). To create the effect of a shadow, darken the section by sliding the gray (gamma) slider to the right; to create the effect of a highlight, move the slider to the left. Click Preview and continue experimenting until you are satisfied with the results. Click OK.

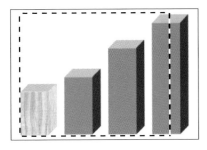

9. To simulate perspective in the side texture, choose Effects from the Image menu and Scale from the submenu. With the pointer over one of the corner boxes, condense the texture horizontally.

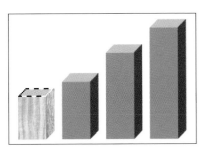

10. Deselect the artwork (⌘D). With the magic wand tool, click the corresponding top section of the column.

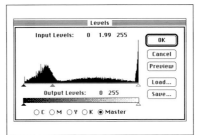

11. Choose Paste Into from the Edit menu; then adjust the color as necessary using the Levels dialog box. Click OK.

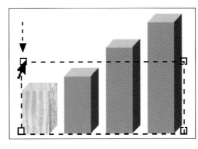

12. If necessary, use the Scale command to scale the texture vertically.

13. Repeat this procedure for each pie slice or column in your chart. When you have finished, you can add type; however, remember that once you've deselected type in Photoshop, it can't be edited or reformatted. For more flexibility with type, you may want to use the Illustrator type tools.

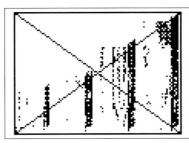

14. To place the Photoshop file in Adobe Illustrator, save the file in EPS format with an 8-bit preview in binary format, and then open an Adobe Illustrator file. Make sure that the Show Placed Images option is turned on in the Preferences dialog box (⌘K). From the File menu, choose Place Art.

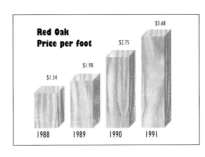

15. Select the type tool, and add the type you want, or copy and paste the type from your original backup file. Because type doesn't always display clearly on top of a placed image, you may want to keep two windows open (one in Artwork mode and one in Preview mode). Preview your work (⌘Y) when you have finished.

5 Text Effects

Glowing text

Software needed: Photoshop 2.0, Adobe Type Manager, Type 1 Fonts

To create glowing text, you use Adobe Photoshop's Border and Feather commands. The size of the border and the amount you feather it varies with the typeface and type size you use. For example, delicate script typefaces require a smaller amount of feathering than some of the heavy sans serif faces. The following table provides recommended Feather and Border values for five very different typefaces at point sizes of 24, 48, 80, and 150. Compare your typeface to the ones in the chart and use the numbers that correspond to the face closest to yours in style and size. Try the procedure using those numbers, and then adjust the numbers to fit your particular needs.*

TYPEFACE	POINT SIZE (PIXELS)	BORDER (PIXELS)	FEATHER (PIXELS)
Bodoni Poster	24	3	2
	48	6	3
	80	10	5
	150	19	10
Künstler Script	24	2	1
	48	4	2
	80	6	3
	150	11	6
Industria Solid	24	2	1
	48	3	1
	80	6	2
	150	12	4
Helvetica Light	24	4	1
	48	7	2
	80	12	3
	150	23	6
Futura Heavy	24	2	2
	48	4	3
	80	6	5
	150	11	10

Top: Typeface: Willow™, 150 points. Border of 13 and feather of 5.
Bottom: Typeface: VAG Rounded Bold. "VAG": 90 points; border of 10 and feather of 3. "Rounded": 30 points; border of 4 and feather of 2.
Right: Typeface: Revue, 60 points. Border of 7 and feather of 5. The selection was loaded again using a border of 7. We then loaded the selection a third time, inverted it, and pressed Delete.

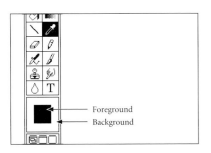

Foreground
Background

1. Open the color image or new RGB document that you want to work on. Double-click the eyedropper tool to set the foreground and background colors to black and white, respectively. This is important because the text must be a solid black in step 3. Choose New Channel from the Mode menu.

2. Select the type tool, and enter the text you want in the new channel. Be sure that you are using Adobe Type Manager and that you have selected the Anti-aliased option in the Type dialog box.

3. Position the text as you want it; then deselect the type (⌘D).

4. From the Image menu, select Map and then Invert (⌘I); this gives you a negative of the image.

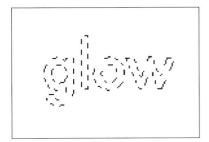

5. Return to the main channel (⌘0), and load your text into this channel by choosing Load Selection from the Select menu.

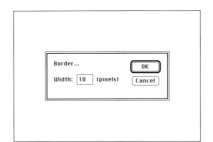

6. With the text still selected, choose Border from the Select menu. Depending on how wide and how intensely colored you want your glow, enter a width value from 3 to 30 pixels in the Border dialog box. (See the table at the beginning of this procedure for guidelines.)

7. Choose Feather from the Select menu, and enter a number between 1 and 10 pixels, depending on how soft and diffused you want the edges of your glow to be. (See the table at the beginning of this procedure for guidelines.)

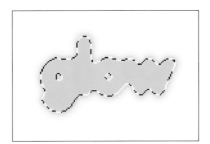

8. Select the foreground color you want to use; then *fill* the glow area with the color (Option-Delete fills the selected area with the foreground color).

9. Choose Load Selection from the Select menu to load the text outline again.

10. Fill the new text with another color; then deselect the image (⌘D).

Shadowed text

Software needed: Adobe Photoshop 2.0, Adobe Type Manager, Type 1 Fonts

Top: The new channel was duplicated twice, using different offset values, Gaussian Blur values, and Levels adjustments for each selection. Typeface: ITC Stone Sans Semibold.
Right: The first selection was loaded and filled with black. We then loaded the second selection, pressed Delete, and filled the area with a color. Next, we inverted the channel containing the first selection, loaded the selection, and filled it with a color. Typeface: Stencil.
Bottom: Typeface: Reporter 2®.

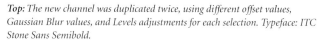

Drop shadows for text, like glowing text outlines, are best created using alpha channels. In this procedure, you apply the Offset and Gaussian Blur filters in an alpha channel to create the shadow. As with glowing text outlines, the values you use in the procedure depend in part on the font you are using. Delicate typefaces at small point sizes require less blurring than heavy faces at large sizes.

1. Open the image that you want to work on. For this example, we used an RGB color document; if you are working in a different color mode, or if you have additional channels in your document, your channel numbers will differ from those used in this procedure.

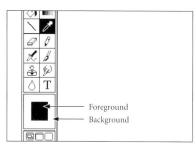

Foreground
Background

2. Double-click the eyedropper tool to set the foreground and background colors to black and white, respectively. This ensures that the text you enter in the alpha channel is solid black. Choose New Channel from the Mode menu to open channel #4.

3. Select the type tool, and enter your text in the new channel. Make sure that you are using Adobe Type Manager and that you have selected the Anti-aliased option in the Type dialog box.

4. Format and kern the text as you want it; then deselect it (⌘D).

5. From the Image menu, choose Map and then Invert (⌘I); this gives you a negative of the image.

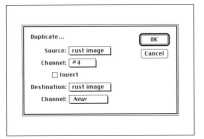

6. Now copy the contents of channel #4 into a new channel, channel #5. Choose Calculate from the Image menu and Duplicate from the submenu. The Source and Destination filenames in the Duplicate dialog box should be the same. The Source Channel should be #4 (the channel containing your text) and the Destination Channel should be *New*. Click OK.

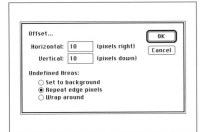

7. Choose Other from the Filter menu and Offset from the submenu. In the Horizontal and Vertical text boxes, enter the size of the shadow in pixels (we entered 10 in both boxes to cast the shadow 10 pixels down and to the right). Select the Repeat Edge Pixels option, and click OK.

8. Apply the Gaussian Blur filter to the same channel. In this example, we used a blur radius of 6 pixels.

9. Return to your main channel (⌘0), and choose Load Selection #5 from the Select menu to load the drop shadow you have just created.

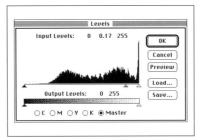

10. Open the Levels dialog box under the Image menu (⌘L), and move the gray (gamma) triangle to the right to darken the shadow. Use the Preview button to check your adjustments.

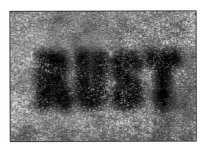

11. Deselect the shadow (⌘D).

12. Load the original text from channel #4 by choosing Load Selection #4 from the Select menu.

13. Fill the selected text with the color of your choice. (Press Option-Delete to fill a selection with the foreground color.) Deselect the text (⌘D).

Variation: For shadows on a white background, follow the same procedure, except darken the shadow area by filling it with some percentage of black.

Translucent shapes

Software needed: Adobe Photoshop 2.0

This technique can be used with any text or object you create or place in an Adobe Photoshop document. You can also use this procedure to create a semi-transparent text container so that columns of text can be incorporated into the image without obscuring the artwork.

Top: *The text container was filled with a custom texture (#15 on page 51) at 60% opacity. The image was then placed in Adobe Illustrator and text was added.*
Left: *Text was entered and positioned in a new channel and then inverted. The selection was then loaded into the original image channel and filled with a blend from orange to yellow with a 50% opacity.*

1. Open the image in which you want the translucent shape. If you are creating a text container that you will use in a page layout program, record the exact size and placement of the shape you need in the page layout program.

2. Draw or place the shape in the image. For a precise rectangle or circle, double-click the appropriate marquee tool and enter the size you want. You can also use type or objects placed from the Adobe Illustrator program.

3. To reposition the selection, hold down the Option and Command keys, and move the cursor inside the selection until the arrow pointer appears; then drag the selection into position. From the Window menu, choose Show Rulers (⌘R) and Show Info, and use the rulers and the Show Info window to help you position the selection.

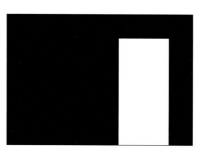

4. Choose Save Selection from the Select menu to save the selection in a new channel.

5. Return to the original image channel (⌘0), and choose Load Selection.

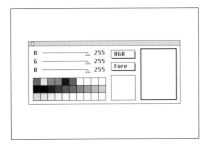

6. Select Show Palette from the Window menu. Choose a foreground color for the translucent area; white or cream work best if you plan to add text to the area.

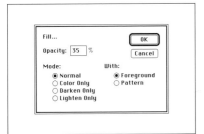

7. Next, use the Fill command in the Edit menu to paint the selection with a tint of the chosen color. In this example, we filled the selection with white at 35% opacity. If you don't like the results, choose Undo from the Edit menu (⌘Z), and try a different opacity.

8. Deselect (⌘D). Save the file in Photoshop format before continuing to the next step.

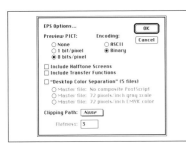

9. If you plan to add text to the area, save the file in EPS format so that the image can be brought into your page layout program. Use the filename suffix *.eps*.

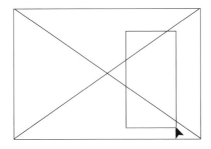

10. Open your page layout program, (we used Illustrator), and place or import the *.eps* file into your page. Using the measurements recorded in step 1, draw and position a text block over the translucent area.

11. Format and paint the text.

〰 *Moving the selection marquee*

To move a selection marquee without affecting the background image, hold down the Command and Option keys, and move the pointer inside the selection until the arrow pointer appears. This lets you click and drag the selection marquee into position without moving the area inside the marquee. Hold down the Shift key as you drag if you want to constrain the movement to the nearest 45-degree angle.

Gradations in type

Software needed: Adobe Illustrator 3, Adobe Type Manager, Type 1 Fonts

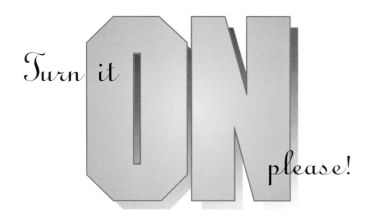

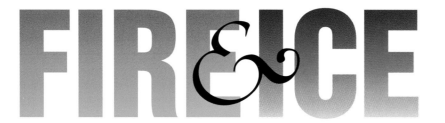

Creating blends inside type is a very memory-intensive process. If your printer is an older model or your computer has only a small amount of RAM, be sure to read the tip at the end of this procedure. You may also want to read the section on creating efficient and smooth blends (page 38) before you use this technique.

1. Using the type tool, create your text. For the best printing results, keep the number of letters to a minimum; if the text is too long, the printer may run out of memory. Format and kern the text.

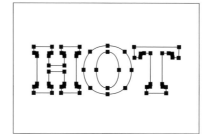

2. Choose the selection tool from the toolbox. Make sure that the text is selected; then choose Create Outlines from the Type menu.

3. Now create a blend exactly the size of your type outlines. Lock the letters (⌘1) so that you can't accidentally move them; then select the pen tool, and draw a horizontal line a little longer than the text. Position the line just above the text.

4. Paint the line (⌘I) the color you want at the top of your blend; use a stroke weight of 2.5 points.

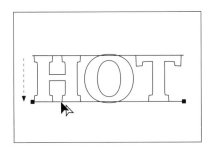

5. To create the bottom line for the blend, begin dragging the top line; then hold down the Option and Shift keys to copy the line and constrain its movement. When the line is positioned just below the bottom edge of the type, release the mouse button and then the Option and Shift keys.

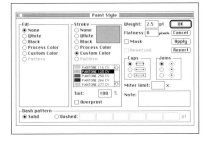

6. Paint the line (⌘I) the color you want at the bottom of your blend; use a stroke weight of 2.5 points.

7. Select the left endpoints of both lines; then select the blend tool. Click one endpoint of the top line and then the corresponding endpoint of the bottom line. Adobe Illustrator enters a recommended number of steps in the Blend dialog box, based on the percentage of color change between the first and last steps in the blend. Click OK.

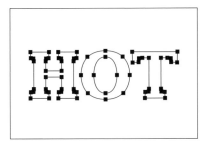

8. Use the selection marquee to select the two lines and the blend, and group them (⌘G). Hide the group (⌘3) so that the type is not obscured. Unlock the type (⌘2).

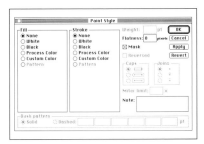

9. For the letterforms to function as a single mask, you must first define them as a compound path by choosing Make Compound from the Paint menu (⌘-Option-G). Next, open the Paint Style dialog box (⌘I), paint the type with a fill and stroke of None, and click the Mask option.

10. Choose Show All from the Arrange menu (⌘4) to redisplay the blend. Use the selection marquee to select both the blend and the type, and group them (⌘G). This prevents the mask from masking other objects in your file.

11. Preview (⌘Y) to check your blend and your layering.

❧ Printing complex paths

Depending on the memory in your computer or printer, you may run into problems printing complex paths like type masks and blends. Here are a few guidelines you can follow to help avoid these problems:

- Use the minimum number of steps needed in your blend. Follow the guidelines described under "Generating Smooth Blends" (pages 38-41).
- Use simple typefaces without complex curves, for example, bold sans serif faces. The more complex the typeface design, the more complex the path.
- Change the flatness setting for the typeface mask in the Paint Style dialog box. Use a flatness of 3 or 4 if you are printing to a high-resolution imagesetter: you won't see any difference in the artwork but it will simplify the path. (See Section 1, "Working Efficiently," for more information on flatness.)
- If your text contains many characters, define each letter as a mask and create a blend for each letter. This gives you more blends and more objects, but simplifies the individual paths. To minimize the number of individual blends, you can also define the blend as a pattern and fill each letter with the pattern.

6 Special Effects

Filter combinations

Software needed: Adobe Photoshop 2.0

Sometimes you want a texture or special effect that can't be achieved with the application of just one filter. Shown here are just a few of the hundreds of combinations you can use to enhance your Adobe Photoshop images. While the examples here illustrate filters applied to the entire image, these combinations can also be applied to just a selected area. To duplicate an effect shown here, apply the filters in the order indicated. Changing the image resolution also lessens or exaggerates the effect. The images below are CMYK files at a resolution of 200 pixels per inch.

ORIGINAL

1. GAUSSIAN BLUR: 2.0
2. DIFFUSE: NORMAL, TWO TIMES

1. FIND EDGES
2. FACET

1. CRYSTALLIZE: 7.0
2. FIND EDGES

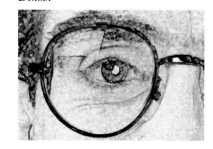
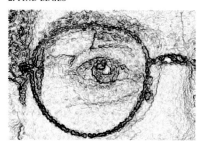

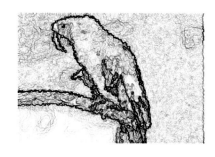

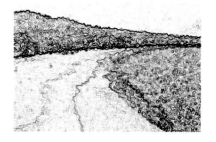

1. MOSAIC: 10
2. RIPPLE: 100, MEDIUM

1. POINTILLIZE: 5
2. FACET: THREE TIMES

1. HIGH PASS: 10
2. DIFFUSE: LIGHTEN ONLY, THREE TIMES

1. ADD NOISE: 70, UNIFORM
2. DESPECKLE

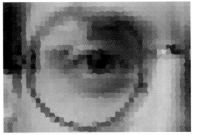
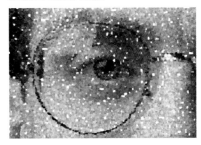
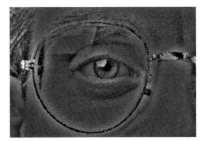
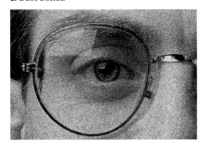

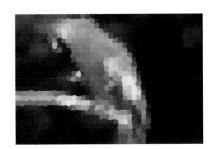

Recessed text and images

Software needed: Adobe Photoshop 2.0

Top Left: The procedure described here was followed using a photograph of tree bark. Typeface: Wood Type Ornaments 2.
Top Right: The procedure described here was followed omitting steps 11 and 12, which were not necessary for this white background. The background was filled with Texture #6 from page 50 at 70% opacity. The shadow areas were filled with the texture twice and then filled with 30% black.
Bottom: Typeface: Künstler Script.

1. Open the file in which you want the recessed image. In this example, we used an RGB image.

2. Choose New Channel from the Mode menu to open a new channel. Select the type tool, and click in the channel to open the Type dialog box. Choose the typeface and size you want, select the Anti-aliased option, and type your text. Click OK, deselect the text (⌘D), and invert the image (⌘I).

3. Return to the RGB channel (⌘0), and choose Load Selection from the Select menu to load selection #4. To reposition the type, hold down the Option and Command keys, and move the cursor inside the selection until the arrow pointer appears; then drag the selection into position.

4. Choose Save Selection to save the selection back to channel #4; this repositions the type in the channel.

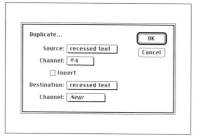

5. From the Image menu, choose Calculate and then Duplicate. In the Duplicate dialog box, make sure that the Destination and Source names are the same, and select *New* for the Destination Channel. Click OK. This copies the type into a new channel (#5).

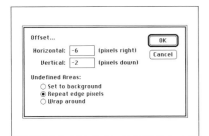

6. In the new channel, choose Other from the Filter menu and Offset from the submenu. Enter the amount you want to offset the type to create a shadowed edge (we used a Horizontal value of −6 and a Vertical value of −2). Select the Repeat Edge Pixels option, and click OK.

7. Return to channel #4 (⌘4) and load selection #5.

8. Choose Inverse from the Select menu to invert the selection; then fill the selection with black. (Double-click the eyedropper tool to change the foreground and background colors to black and white, respectively; then press Option-Delete to fill the selection.) You now have a mask for the recessed area. Deselect everything (⌘D).

9. Letters and images with sharp corners may need a little touch-up work to smooth out the edges of the mask. Zoom in on the image, and use the paint brush to fill any extra white areas with black. For the best results, use a small brush.

10. Return to channel #5 (⌘5), and load selection #4. Fill the selection with black (Option-Delete); to create a mask for the dark shadow. Because the next step in the procedure distorts the image, save the image now; this enables you to restore the image and the two masks at any time by choosing the Revert command.

11. With selection #4 still active, return to the original image channel (⌘0). Press ⌘F to apply the last filter to the selection; this offsets the selection using the same Offset filter values used in step 6.

12. Choose Blur from the Filter menu and Blur More from the submenu. The effect is subtle; however, blurring the selection helps create the impression of depth. Hide the selection edges (⌘H) so that you can more easily see the effect.

13. To create more depth, fill the hidden selection with a percentage of black (we used 50%), or use the Levels dialog box (⌘L) to darken the selected area.

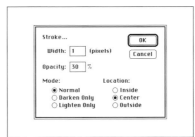

14. Use the Stroke command in the Edit menu to give the edges of the selection more definition. In this example, we used a stroke width of 1 pixel and an opacity of 30%. Select the Normal Mode option and the Center Location option. Click OK.

15. To create a shadow along one of the edges, load selection #5. Use the Feather command in the Select menu to add a 1-pixel feather edge; then fill the selection with black (Option-Delete). Deselect (⌘D) to view the results.

Embossing

Software needed: Adobe Photoshop 2.0, Adobe Illustrator 3 (optional)

1. Open the file in which you wish to create embossed graphics. For the best results, use a textured surface.

2. Choose New Channel from the Mode menu to create a new, blank channel (#4).

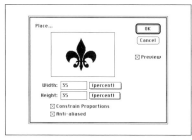

3. Copy or create the object you want to emboss in the new channel. In this example, we used the Place command to place an Adobe Illustrator file at the desired size. The object you use in this procedure should be painted with only 100% black (no tints) and white.

4. Position the object in the image area; then deselect it (⌘D).

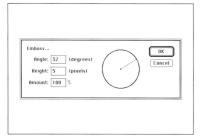

5. Choose Stylize from the Filter menu and Emboss from the submenu. Enter the desired Angle, Height, and Amount. In most cases, an Amount of 100% gives the best results.

Top: The Japanese characters were embossed using a photograph of fibrous paper. Typeface: Ryumin Light-KL.
Right: A color photograph was converted to Bitmap mode and copied to a new channel. The contrast was boosted using the Levels dialog box. The image was embossed using Texture #18 from page 51.
Bottom: The image of the lion was embossed using a photograph of metal.

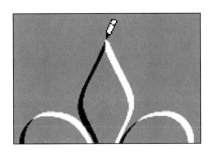

6. Letters and images with sharp corners may need a little touch-up work to smooth out the edges. Zoom in on the image, and use the pencil tool with a foreground color of black or white to bring the corners of the image to a point.

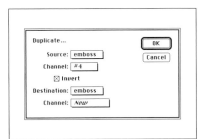

7. Choose Calculate from the Image menu and Duplicate from the submenu. In the Duplicate dialog box, make sure that the Destination and Source names are the same, and select *New* for the Destination Channel. Select Invert; then click OK. You now have two embossed objects: one in channel #4, highlighted on the right side, and one in channel #5, highlighted on the left side.

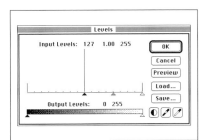

8. Use the Levels dialog box under the Image menu (⌘L) to isolate the highlights in channel #5, making all other values solid black. To do this, drag the black Input Levels triangle to the center of the histogram, until the value reads 127, then click OK.

9. Open channel #4 (⌘4), and repeat step 8. The result should look like the picture shown here.

10. Return to the original image channel (⌘0), and load selection #4. This selection represents the highlights of your embossed object. Hide the selection edges (⌘H) so that you will be able to clearly see the color change in the next step.

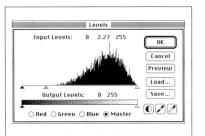

11. Open the Levels dialog box (⌘L), and move the gray midtone triangle to the left to make the selected area lighter. Use the Preview button to check your adjustments; when you are satisfied with the effect, click OK.

12. Load selection #5. This selection represents the shadows of your embossed object. Hide the selection edges (⌘H).

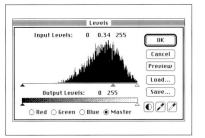

13. Open the Levels dialog box (⌘L), and move the gray midtone triangle to the right to darken the selection. When you are satisfied with the results, click OK.

14. Deselect (⌘D).

Posterizing photographs

Software needed: Adobe Photoshop 2.0

If you've tried using the Adobe Photoshop Posterize command to posterize color images, you've probably produced some unexpected results. It's important to know that Photoshop posterizes each channel of an image. This means that a 2-level posterization produces two colors in each channel of an image, generating a total of 8 colors in an RGB image (2 x 2 x 2) and 16 colors in a CMYK image. The technique described here provides an alternative way to create color posterizations that gives you more control over the number of colors as well as the colors themselves. This procedure lends itself well to process or custom color inks.

1. Open the file you want to posterize. If it is a color file, convert it to Gray Scale mode. Note that the file should be sized and cropped before you posterize; resizing after you posterize adds more gray levels to the file.

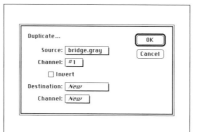

2. From the Image menu, choose Calculate and then Duplicate. Click OK. This creates a copy of the file so that you can freely experiment with different colors and levels of posterization.

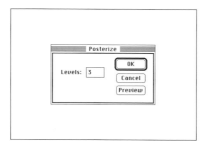

3. Choose Map from the Image menu and Posterize from the submenu (⌘J). Enter the number of colors you want in your final file (we used 3). Click OK.

4. Now remove any unwanted detail or awkward shapes from your image. To do this, select the paint brush; then hold down the Option key to access the eyedropper, and select the color of gray in the image that you want to paint with. Use the paint brush to paint over the unwanted area. (In this example, we removed the small cloud.)

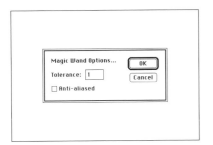

5. To add color to the image, convert the image to RGB mode. Double-click the magic wand tool. Set the Tolerance to 1, and turn off the Anti-aliased option. This causes the magic wand tool to select only pixels with exactly the same color value as the pixel you click.

6. Click one of the black areas in the image; then choose Similar from the Select menu. All the black in the image should be selected.

7. Choose Show Palette from the Window menu. (See the tip at the end of this procedure for instructions on building a color palette.) Select the color that you want to fill the darkest shadow areas of your image, and fill the selection (Option-Delete). To hide the selection marquee, choose Hide Edges from the Select menu (⌘H).

8. Now use the magic wand tool to select the next darkest level of gray, and choose Similar from the Select menu.

9. Fill the selection with the next color in your palette.

10. Repeat steps 8-9 for each remaining gray level in your image.

❧ Building a color palette for color posterization

When colorizing an image, it helps to build a color palette for the image before you start. To do this, use the eyedropper tool to sample each of the gray levels in the grayscale image, adding each gray to the color palette (hold down the Option key to add colors to the palette). Fill the swatch below each gray in the palette with the color you will use to replace the gray.

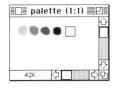

To create a palette that you can save and reuse, open a new RGB file. (A file size of 100 x 100 pixels and a resolution of 72 ppi should be large enough for the palette.) Select the paint brush tool. Option-click each of the grays in the image, and paint a small swatch of each gray at the top of the palette file. To represent white on a white background, draw a small box and stroke it with 1 pixel of black.

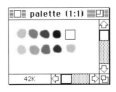

Under each gray level, paint a small swatch of the color you will use to replace that gray. Save the palette using the name of the artwork file with which you will use the palette and the filename suffix *.palette*.

Posterize-style illustrations

Software needed: Adobe Photoshop 2.0, Adobe Illustrator 3

This style of illustration lends itself well to printing with custom colors. Reminiscent of early 20th century German poster art, the drawings are made up of flat, simplified shapes. You start with an existing photograph, simplify it, and then trace it. Two versions of this procedure are provided: the first, the "professional method," requires some drawing ability and a scanner. If you can't draw or don't have a scanner, try the second method. The results are less predictable, but the computer does most of the work for you.

Professional method

1. Open the Adobe Photoshop file you want to use as a basis for your illustration. If it is a color file, convert it to Gray Scale mode.

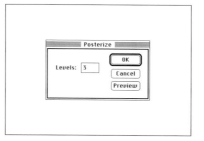

2. From the Image menu, choose Map and then Posterize (⌘J). Posterize the artwork using 2-4 levels. Use the Preview button to examine the results of different levels, and choose the one that retains the shapes and shadow areas that you want in your final illustration.

3. Now print the file on a laser printer along with the original grayscale file. Compare the two printouts, and outline the shapes you want in the final drawing. This step is necessary because when the computer posterizes, it may leave out some important shapes or details and save some unimportant ones. This step requires some drawing experience.

4. Place tracing paper over your posterized print, and trace the shapes by outlining them with a black, fine-point pen. If you anticipate making many changes or corrections, use a pencil, and then trace over the final drawing with a pen. (You will scan this drawing, and pencil may not be picked up as well by the scanner.)

5. Now scan the drawing. Save it in PICT format so that you can trace it in Adobe Illustrator. (If you want to first autotrace the drawing using Adobe Streamline, save the scan in TIFF format.) Open the file in Adobe Illustrator.

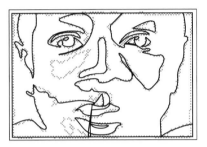

6. Using the PICT file as a template, trace the outlines with the pen tool. Keep in mind that shapes in Illustrator are like layers of colored paper. Instead of creating "puzzle piece" shapes and trying to align them, make the background a solid rectangle, and then create the image shapes on top of it.

7. Add color to the shapes using the Paint Style dialog box (⌘I). Preview your work (⌘Y). If some shapes need work, go back to Artwork and Template mode (⌘E), and adjust the curves.

Non-drawing Method

1. Follow steps 1 and 2 of the previous procedure. Double-click the magic wand tool. Set the Tolerance to 1, and turn off the Anti-aliased option. This ensures that only one color at a time will be selected. Open the General Preferences dialog box (⌘K), and set the Path Tolerance to 4 pixels.

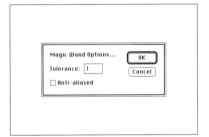

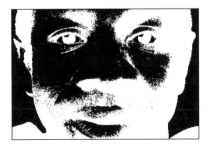

2. Click one of the black areas in the image; then choose Similar from the Select menu. All the black in the image should be selected. Choose Save Selection from the Select menu.

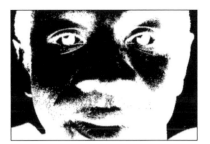

3. Apply the Blur filter to the new channel twice. This softens the edges of the shapes and removes unwanted detail.

4. Return to the main image channel (⌘1), and load the selection; then choose Make Path from the Select menu. Because the path tolerance has been set to 4, this step will smooth the curves a bit. For even softer, more generalized curves, click inside each path to make it a selection; then choose Make Path again.

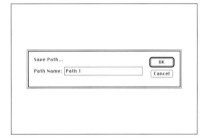

5. Choose Save Path from the Pen menu; then exit pen mode (⌘D). Repeat steps 2-5 for all the white areas and then all the gray areas in the image. When you have finished, you will have saved a path for each gray level in your posterization.

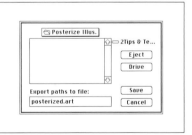

6. Now export the paths to Adobe Illustrator; this step is necessary to ensure sharp-edged (non-anti-aliased) paths. From the File menu, choose Export and then Paths to Illustrator. Photoshop automatically gives the file the same name as the old file with a suffix of *.art* to indicate that it's an Illustrator file. Save the file.

7. Open the file in Illustrator. Add color to the shapes using the Paint Style dialog box (⌘I). Preview your work (⌘Y). If some shapes need work, go back to Artwork and Template mode (⌘E), and adjust the curves.

Creating a rustic or eroded effect

Software needed: Adobe Photoshop 2.0, Adobe Illustrator 3, Adobe Type Manager, Type 1 Fonts

Some artists try to simulate an eroded or weathered effect with their type or artwork by making a series of photocopies in which each copy is made from the previous copy. The following technique lets you achieve a similar look with more control and far less paper. Use the chart below to estimate how eroded you want your image to be before you start. Notice that the effect varies dramatically at different resolutions.

Top: *We created the file in Adobe Illustrator using a border from Adobe Collector's Edition. We then opened it in Adobe Photoshop (300 ppi) and applied the Diffuse filter once using the Normal option and once using the Lighten Only option. Typefaces: Caslon Open Face, Adobe Caslon Expert, and a character from Adobe Wood Type™ Ornaments.*

Left: *We opened a 200 ppi file in Photoshop and applied the Diffuse filter twice using the Normal option. We then selected the deer and applied the filter four more times. Typeface: Lithos™.*

Right: *We created the file in Illustrator using the multiple-outline technique described on page 10. We then opened the file in Photoshop (200 ppi) and applied the Diffuse filter using the Lighten Only option. We used the enhancement technique described at the end of this procedure and then diffused the file twice more using the Normal option.*

DIFFUSE AMOUNT	PHOTOSHOP RESOLUTION (PIXELS PER INCH)		
	100 PPI	200 PPI	300 PPI
NONE	Aa	Aa	Aa
DIFFUSE ONE TIME NORMAL	Aa	Aa	Aa
DIFFUSE TWO TIMES NORMAL	Aa	Aa	Aa
DIFFUSE THREE TIMES NORMAL	Aa	Aa	Aa
DIFFUSE TEN TIMES NORMAL	Aa	Aa	Aa
DIFFUSE TWO TIMES LIGHTEN	Aa	Aa	Aa
DIFFUSE FIVE TIMES LIGHTEN	A	Aa	Aa
DIFFUSE TWO TIMES DARKEN	Aa	Aa	Aa
DIFFUSE FIVE TIMES DARKEN	Aa	Aa	Aa

1. Create an image using Adobe Illustrator, and paint it as desired. (In general, this effect works best on large headlines or artwork.) Preview (⌘Y) to check your work; then save the file.

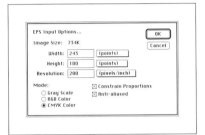

2. Open the file in Adobe Photoshop. Photoshop automatically opens color Illustrator files in CMYK mode, with the paths anti-aliased. Refer to the chart at left to determine the desired resolution for the file.

3. Save the file with a suffix of *.diffused*. Be careful to use Save As instead of Save so that the Adobe Photoshop file doesn't replace your original Adobe Illustrator file. You'll want to preserve the original so that you can try out variations of this technique.

4. From the Filter menu, choose Stylize and then Diffuse. Choose the Diffuse Mode option you want (see the chart on the facing page for examples). Using the Lighten Only option creates the effect of the image dissolving; using the Darken Only option creates the effect of the image spreading. Click OK.

5. Depending on the intensity of the effect you want, reapply the filter (⌘F). In this example, we applied the filter three times.

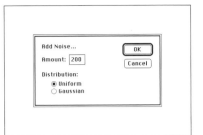

Enhancement: To give some texture to the inner areas of the image where the diffusion might not have reached, create a texture channel to combine with the artwork. Choose New Channel from the Mode menu, and add texture using the Add Noise filter. In the Add Noise dialog box, enter 200 for the Amount, and select the Uniform option. Click OK.

Invert the Channel (⌘I).

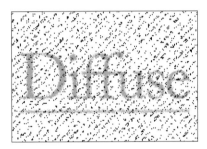

Return to the CMYK channel (⌘0), and choose Load Selection from the Select menu. If you want to hide the selection edges, choose Hide Edges from the Select menu (⌘H).

Now fill the selection with the background color. If the background color displayed in the toolbox is different from the background color in the image, choose the eyedropper tool, and Option-click the background image color to make them the same; then press Delete to fill the selection with the color.

Composite photographs

Software needed: Adobe Photoshop 2.0

This is a simplified version of the matte technique called blue-screen composite that is used in the video and film industries to place a subject from one piece of film into another. While there are many ways to do this in Adobe Photoshop, this technique will give you the most flawless results. For a blue-screen composite, the subject is photographed against a background that shares no colors with it. Because the subject in video is usually a person, blue or green is often the chosen background color. Before you start, analyze the colors in your subject, and determine what color will be best to photograph it against. Because you will remove the background electronically, it's important to make sure that the subject doesn't contain any of that color.

1. Photograph your subject image. For still photography, use a medium blue backdrop that contains little to no red (we used a sheet of uncoated PANTONE* 279). If there are shadows in the photograph that you want to use as the composite background, the subject should be lighted from the same direction as the background. Open the subject RGB file in Adobe Photoshop.

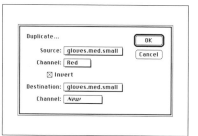

2. Now generate a matte using the red and blue channels of the image. (A *matte* is an image that is white in the area of the subject and black in the background.) From the Image menu, choose Calculate and then Duplicate. Click the Invert option, and duplicate the red channel into a new channel of the same image.

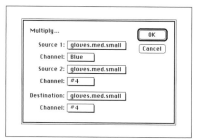

3. You create the matte by "sandwiching" this new channel with the blue channel. To do this, choose Calculate from the Image menu and Multiply from the submenu. Multiply the blue channel by channel #4, and put the result back into channel #4. The Source and Destination filenames should be the same. Compare your screen closely with this dialog box illustration.

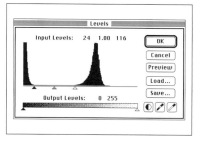

4. Adjust the densities of the matte using the Levels dialog box under the Image menu (⌘L). Drag the white (highlights) Input Levels triangle to the left of the right spike in the histogram, and drag the black (shadows) triangle to the right of the left spike. The triangles should be positioned as shown in this figure. Click OK.

5. Invert the channel (⌘I). This creates the matte.

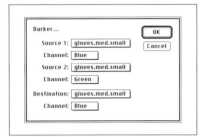

6. You now need to adjust for any partially transparent areas of the matte (such as a person's hair) that would allow some blue screen color to show through. To do this, choose Darker from the Calculate menu. Choose the green and blue channels as the source channels and the blue channel as the destination channel.

7. Return to the RGB channel of your image (⌘0). The blue areas of your image will have a green cast.

8. Choose Load Selection from the Select menu to select the subject, and copy it to the Clipboard (⌘C).

9. Open the background file for the composite image. Paste the subject (⌘V), and move it into position. Before deselecting the subject, make any other adjustments to help integrate the subject with the background. You can adjust the selection's color, scale it, rotate it, or use any other Photoshop editing feature while the selection is still "floating."

Enhancement: One way to help your subject blend into the new background is to create a shadow. To do this, choose Inverse from the Select menu after you paste the selection onto the background in step 9. This lets you mask the subject while painting — just as an airbrush artist uses frisket to protect certain areas when airbrushing. Save the file before you begin painting.

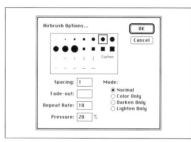

Double-click the airbrush tool. Choose a small to medium brush size and a pressure of 25% or less. Rather than creating the shadow in one step, you will build up the shadow by painting several thin layers of black spray. This gives you greater control and lets you create a more subtle effect.

Hide the edges of the selection (⌘H); then zoom in to work on small areas. Create your shadow carefully by laying down one thin layer of paint and then painting over it again to darken the areas closest to the subject. Create the strokes in one direction, and then go back over them instead of brushing back and forth. This makes it easier to undo mistakes.

For the best results, the shadows should appear consistent with any existing shadows on the original subject photograph.

7

Duotones, Tritones, and Quadtones

Creating duotones, tritones, and quadtones

Duotones

Tritones

Quadtones

Creating duotones, tritones, and quadtones

Software needed: Adobe Photoshop 2.0

Adobe Photoshop 2.0 provides the ability to create monotones, duotones, tritones, and quadtones. Monotones are grayscale images printed with a single, non-black ink. Duotones, tritones, and quadtones are grayscale images printed with two, three, and four inks, respectively. In these images, different colored inks are used to reproduce different levels of gray rather than to reproduce different colors.

Duotones, tritones, and quadtones have been used for years by designers to increase the tonal range of grayscale images. While a grayscale photographic reproduction can reproduce up to 256 levels of gray, a single plate on a printing press can reproduce only about 50 levels of gray. The use of two, three, or four inks to print a grayscale image, therefore, significantly increases the number of gray levels that can be reproduced. The results are a dramatic improvement in the reproduction of subtle detail and in the overall quality of the image.

A typical duotone uses a black ink to capture the shadow detail in an image and a gray or colored ink for the midtone and highlight areas. In Adobe Photoshop, you specify how each ink is distributed across the shadow and highlight areas of the image using the Duotone Curve dialog box. This dialog box displays a curve, similar to the transfer function used by Photoshop to compensate for dot gain or loss by the imagesetter. The duotone transfer curve maps each grayscale value on the original image to the actual ink percentage that will be used to print the image. So, for example, if you enter 70 in the 100% text box, a 70% dot of that ink color will be used to print the 100% shadow areas of the image. Keep in mind that you specify a duotone curve for each of the inks used to print a duotone, tritone, or quadtone image.

The following pages show some examples of duotones, tritones, and quadtones created in Adobe Photoshop using Pantone® black and various shades of gray or color. The duotone curves used to determine the distribution of each ink were created by specifying only three to six points on the curve. While the Duotone Curve function allows you to specify up to 13 points on the graph, if you specify fewer points, Photoshop automatically calculates the intermediate values.

Each of the examples shown here also includes the overprint colors specified in Adobe Photoshop for the image. The Overprint Colors feature allows you to tell Photoshop exactly what colors result when the various combination of inks are overlayed so that the program can accurately display the image. To do this, you simply select the color you want to change

from the Overprint Colors dialog box, and adjust the color values until the color looks as it should. Note that this adjustment affects only your screen display and not your final output.

A final consideration when creating duotones is that both the order in which the inks are printed and the screen angles you use will have a dramatic affect on your final output. In general, to ensure the most fully saturated colors, darker inks should be printed before lighter inks. For selecting the optimal screen angles, a good rule of thumb is to set the screen angles 30 degrees apart; if you are printing a quadtone, the final (lightest) ink should be offset at 15 degrees. If you are using Adobe Photoshop version 2.0.1 or later, use the Auto button in the Halftone Screens dialog box. If your output device is equipped with PostScript Level 2, click the Accurate Screens option before clicking OK in the Auto Screens dialog box.

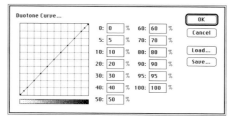

The Duotone Curve dialog box allows you to specify the distribution of each ink by specifying density (i.e., dot size) adjustments for up to 13 points on the curve. The curve shown here is a "linear" curve, where each grayscale value from the original image is mapped to the same density value of the given ink. This means that a 10% gray on the original image will be printed with a 10% density value of the given ink, a 90% gray will be printed with a 90% density of the ink, and so on.

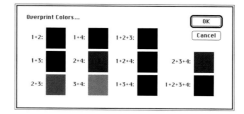

To make sure that Photoshop accurately displays overprint colors on-screen, select the overprint color you want to modify, and then adjust the color values until the color appears correct. If possible, use a printed sample of the overprinted inks to ensure the most accurate screen display. Before adjusting colors on-screen, it is important that you have accurately calibrated your system according to the instructions provided in Chapter 15 of the Photoshop user guide.

Duotones

Printing specifications:
175 line screen / 2400 dpi imagesetter

Screen angles:
Ink 1: 45°   Ink 2: 15°

Printing Inks:

 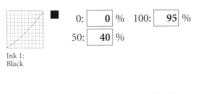

Ink 1:
Black

Ink 2:
PMS Cool Gray 10

Overprint Color:

Ink 1+2

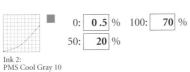 0: **0** %   100: **95** %
50: **40** %

Ink 1:
Black

0: **0.5** %   100: **70** %
50: **20** %

Ink 2:
PMS Cool Gray 10

0: **0** %   70: **40** %
40: **14.4** %   100: **98** %

Ink 1:
Black

0: **0.5** %   100: **80** %
50: **50** %

Ink 2:
PMS Cool Gray 10

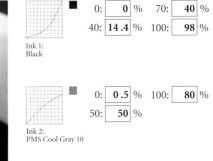

0: **0** %   80: **60** %
50: **30** %   100: **95** %

Ink 1:
Black

0: **0.5** %   100: **95** %
50: **40** %

Ink 2:
PMS Cool Gray 10

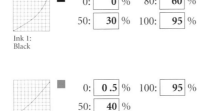

0: **0** %   80: **55** %
30: **4** %   100: **95** %
50: **16** %

Ink 1:
Black

0: **0.5** %   50: **60** %
20: **32** %   100: **85** %

Ink 2:
PMS Cool Gray 10

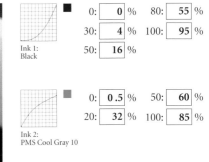

Duotones

Printing specifications:
175 line screen / 2400 dpi imagesetter

Screen angles:
Ink 1: 45°   Ink 2: 15°

Printing Inks:

Ink 1:
Black

Ink 2:
PMS 485

Overprint Color:

Ink 1+2

Ink 1:
Black

	0:	0	%	100:	98	%
	50:	45	%			

Ink 2:
PMS 485

	0:	0.5	%	100:	55	%
	50:	15	%			

Ink 1:
Black

	0:	0	%	50:	30	%
	5:	3	%	100:	95	%

Ink 2:
PMS 485

	0:	0	%	100:	80	%
	50:	35	%			

Ink 1:
Black

	0:	0	%	100:	98	%
	50:	40	%			

Ink 2:
PMS 485

	0:	0	%	100:	78	%
	50:	25	%			

Ink 1:
Black

	0:	0	%	80:	60	%
	5:	3	%	100:	100	%
	40:	20	%			

Ink 2:
PMS 485

	0:	0	%	50:	45	%
	5:	5	%	100:	90	%

Tritones

Printing specifications:
175 line screen / 2400 dpi imagesetter

Screen angles:
Ink 1: 45°   Ink 2: 15°   Ink 3: 75°

Printing Inks:

Ink 1:
Black

Ink 2:
PMS Cool Gray 10

Ink 3:
PMS Cool Gray 1

Overprint Colors:

Ink 1+2

Ink 1+3

Ink 2+3

Ink 1+2+3

SOFT

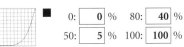

0:	**0** %	80:	**40** %
50:	**5** %	100:	**100** %

Ink 1:
Black

0:	**0** %	50:	**30.5** %
20:	**12** %	100:	**95** %

Ink 2:
PMS Cool Gray 10

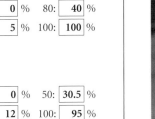

0:	**0** %	100:	**100** %
40:	**73.8** %		

Ink 3:
PMS Cool Gray 1

NORMAL

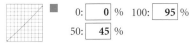

0:	**0** %	80:	**40** %
30:	**5** %	90:	**67** %
50:	**10** %	100:	**100** %

Ink 1:
Black

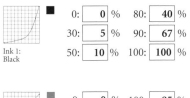

0:	**0** %	100:	**95** %
50:	**45** %		

Ink 2:
PMS Cool Gray 10

0:	**0** %	100:	**100** %
40:	**74** %		

Ink 3:
PMS Cool Gray 1

LOW CONTRAST

0:	**0** %	50:	**10** %
30:	**2** %	100:	**70** %

Ink 1:
Black

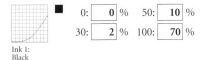

0:	**5** %	100:	**80** %
50:	**20** %		

Ink 2:
PMS Cool Gray 10

0:	**10** %	100:	**100** %
50:	**80** %		

Ink 3:
PMS Cool Gray 1

DARK

0:	**0** %	80:	**60** %
30:	**5** %	90:	**80** %
50:	**20** %	100:	**100** %

Ink 1:
Black

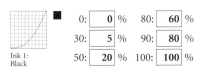

0:	**0** %	100:	**95** %
50:	**40** %		

Ink 2:
PMS Cool Gray 10

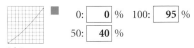

0:	**0** %	100:	**100** %
40:	**74** %		

Ink 3:
PMS Cool Gray 1

Quadtones

Printing specifications:
175 line screen / 2400 dpi imagesetter

Screen angles:
Ink 1: 45°   Ink 2: 15°   Ink 3: 75°   Ink 4: 0°

Printing Inks:

Ink 1:
Black

Ink 2:
PMS Cool Gray 10

Ink 3:
PMS Cool Gray 4

Ink 4:
PMS Cool Gray 1

Overprint Colors:

Ink 1+2   Ink 1+3   Ink 2+3   Ink 1+4   Ink 2+4   Ink 3+4

Ink 1+2+3   Ink 1+2+4   Ink 1+3+4   Ink 2+3+4   Ink 1+2+3+4

SOFT

Ink 1:
Black

0: **0** %   80: **35** %
50: **5** %   100: **100** %

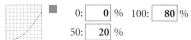
Ink 2:
PMS Cool Gray 10

0: **0** %   100: **80** %
50: **20** %

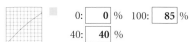
Ink 3:
PMS Cool Gray 4

0: **0** %   100: **85** %
40: **40** %

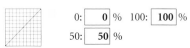
Ink 4:
PMS Cool Gray 1

0: **0** %   100: **100** %
50: **50** %

LOW CONTRAST

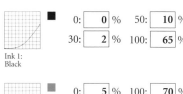
Ink 1:
Black

0: **0** %   50: **10** %
30: **2** %   100: **65** %

Ink 2:
PMS Cool Gray 10

0: **5** %   100: **70** %
50: **20** %

Ink 3:
PMS Cool Gray 4

0: **10** %   100: **70** %
40: **25** %

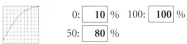
Ink 4:
PMS Cool Gray 1

0: **10** %   100: **100** %
50: **80** %

NORMAL

Ink 1:
Black

0: **0** %   80: **40** %
50: **5** %   100: **100** %

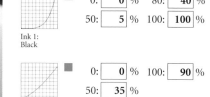
Ink 2:
PMS Cool Gray 10

0: **0** %   100: **90** %
50: **35** %

Ink 3:
PMS Cool Gray 4

0: **0** %   100: **90** %
40: **45** %

Ink 4:
PMS Cool Gray 1

0: **0** %   50: **70** %
5: **10** %   100: **100** %

DARK

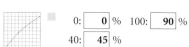
Ink 1:
Black

0: **0** %   80: **40** %
50: **5** %   100: **100** %

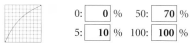
Ink 2:
PMS Cool Gray 10

0: **0** %   100: **90** %
50: **45** %

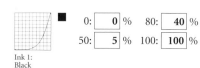
Ink 3:
PMS Cool Gray 4

0: **0** %   100: **90** %
40: **60** %

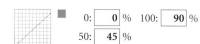
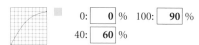

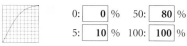
Ink 4:
PMS Cool Gray 1

0: **0** %   50: **80** %
5: **10** %   100: **100** %

Quadtones

Printing specifications:
175 line screen / 2400 dpi imagesetter

Screen angles:
Ink 1: 45°   Ink 2: 15°   Ink 3: 75°   Ink 4: 0°

Printing Inks:

Ink 1:
Black

Ink 2:
PMS 485

Ink 3:
PMS Cool Gray 4

Ink 4:
PMS Cool Gray 1

Overprint Colors:

Ink 1+2   Ink 1+3   Ink 2+3   Ink 1+4   Ink 2+4   Ink 3+4

Ink 1+2+3   Ink 1+2+4   Ink 1+3+4   Ink 2+3+4   Ink 1+2+3+4

Ink 1:
Black

| 0: | 0 % | 80: | 45 % |
| 50: | 10 % | 100: | 100 % |

Ink 2:
PMS 485

| 0: | 0 % | 70: | 25 % |
| 30: | 5 % | 100: | 60 % |

Ink 3:
PMS Cool Gray 4

| 0: | 0 % | 100: | 100 % |
| 40: | 65 % | | |

Ink 4:
PMS Cool Gray 1

| 0: | 0 % | 50: | 80 % |
| 5: | 5 % | 100: | 100 % |

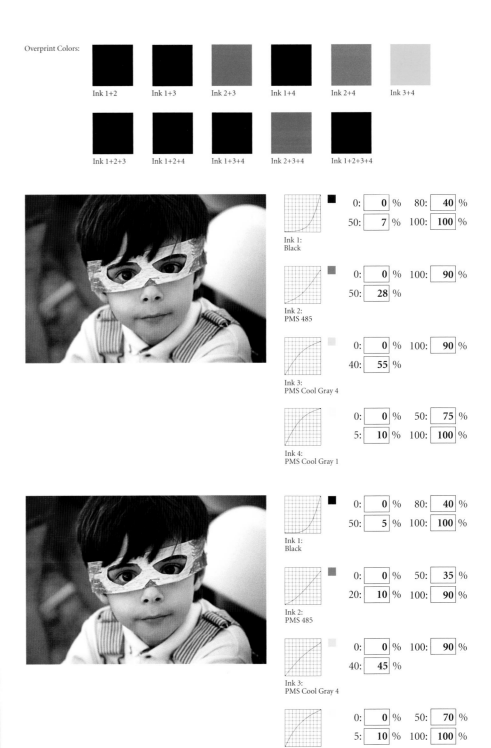

Ink 1:
Black

| 0: | 0 % | 80: | 40 % |
| 50: | 7 % | 100: | 100 % |

Ink 2:
PMS 485

| 0: | 0 % | 100: | 90 % |
| 50: | 28 % | | |

Ink 3:
PMS Cool Gray 4

| 0: | 0 % | 100: | 90 % |
| 40: | 55 % | | |

Ink 4:
PMS Cool Gray 1

| 0: | 0 % | 50: | 75 % |
| 5: | 10 % | 100: | 100 % |

Ink 1:
Black

| 0: | 0 % | 80: | 40 % |
| 50: | 8 % | 100: | 100 % |

Ink 2:
PMS 485

| 0: | 0 % | 70: | 38 % |
| 30: | 9 % | 100: | 80 % |

Ink 3:
PMS Cool Gray 4

| 0: | 0 % | 100: | 100 % |
| 40: | 60 % | | |

Ink 4:
PMS Cool Gray 1

| 0: | 0 % | 50: | 80 % |
| 5: | 10 % | 100: | 100 % |

Ink 1:
Black

| 0: | 0 % | 80: | 40 % |
| 50: | 5 % | 100: | 100 % |

Ink 2:
PMS 485

| 0: | 0 % | 50: | 35 % |
| 20: | 10 % | 100: | 90 % |

Ink 3:
PMS Cool Gray 4

| 0: | 0 % | 100: | 90 % |
| 40: | 45 % | | |

Ink 4:
PMS Cool Gray 1

| 0: | 0 % | 50: | 70 % |
| 5: | 10 % | 100: | 100 % |

8 Printing and Production

Stereoscopic images

Halftoning

Color trapping and overprinting

Stereoscopic images

Software needed: Adobe Photoshop 2.0

Stereoscopic, or three-dimensional, images achieve the effect of depth by superimposing two slightly offset versions of an image in such a way that each eye sees only one image. You can use Adobe Photoshop to create a type of stereo image, called an anaglyph. *This type of image relies on the principles of color separation to filter the information that is sent to each eye. To achieve the effect, the viewer wears "3-D glasses" that filter the red information in one eye and the blue information in the other. (A pair of these glasses is included in the back of the book.) For this technique, images must be in focus and in RGB mode.*

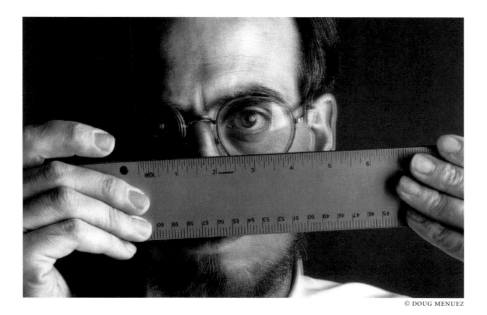

© DOUG MENUEZ

© STEVE KRONGARD

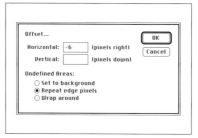

Creating two levels of depth

1. Open the RGB image that you want to use. Save the file with a suffix of *.3d* for easy identification. Do not save this file again until you have completed the entire procedure. If you do, see the tip at the end of the procedure for how to restore all or part of the original image.

2. Go to the red channel (⌘1).

3. From the Filter menu, select Other and then Offset. Enter a negative Horizontal value. This number corresponds to the amount of depth that will be seen in your image. The value you choose will vary with the image: images with well-defined edges require less offsetting than images with soft edges. Select the Repeat Edge Pixels option, and click OK.

4. Return to the RGB channel (⌘0). Double-click the rubber stamp tool to open the dialog box. Select a medium brush size and click the Revert option. Click OK.

5. Now use the rubber stamp tool to restore the original version of the image in those areas that you want to appear in the foreground. For greater precision, press the Caps Lock key to turn the pointer into a cross hair.

6. Put on your 3-D glasses (blue on the right eye and red on left) to see the effect. If necessary, touch up the artwork while wearing the glasses to remove the double images.

Creating three levels of depth

1. Follow steps 1-4 of the previous technique. In step 5, revert the areas of the image that you want to appear in the midground of the 3-D image instead of in the foreground. In this procedure, you will create three, instead of two, levels of depth: you'll create the third level by offsetting the image a positive amount so that it pops out into the foreground.

2. Reopen the original image, and duplicate it into a new file; then close the original image.

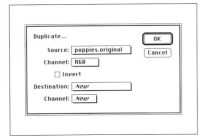

3. Go to the red channel (⌘1) of the Untitled image, and offset the channel using a positive Horizontal value. Offsetting the image to the right brings the image forward when the 3-D glasses are on. Select the Repeat Edge Pixels option, and click OK. Save the image with a suffix of *.foreground* for easy identification.

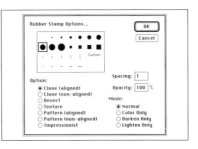

4. Return to the RGB channel (⌘0). Double-click the rubber stamp tool, and select the Clone (aligned) option. Click OK.

5. Move the *.foreground* image so that you can see the *.3d* image window. With the rubber stamp tool still selected, Option-click a clearly recognizable spot in the *.foreground* image that you want to appear in the foreground of the stereo image. You will need to click this spot again in the next step.

6. Click the *.3d* image to make it the active window; then position the pointer on the same spot you clicked in step 5, and drag to begin cloning the *.foreground* image into the *.3d* image.

7. When you have finished cloning in the foreground, put on the 3-D glasses to check your work. You should now see three distinct levels of depth.

❧ *Cloning the original image*

If you have saved a file while you are working so that you can no longer use the Revert option to restore the image, you can still restore the image using the Clone option. To do this, open the original image and use the rubber stamp tool with the Clone option to sample the image; then drag through the image you are working on to "clone in" the original image. When sampling the original image, be sure to click an easily identifiable point in the area you want to restore; to get an exact match when you clone the image, you must begin dragging from precisely the same point in the second image.

Halftoning

Software needed: Adobe Photoshop 2.0, Adobe Illustrator 3 (optional)

You can create a halftone effect using a variety of shapes for the halftone dots, including lines, squares, crosses, and patterns from Adobe Photoshop and Adobe Illustrator. You control both the size and the intensity of the halftone screen. Note that a halftone screen differs from a simple screen in that the size of dots in a halftone screen varies with the density of color. For a plain screening effect, use the Calculate/Screen command under the Image menu.

The pages following this technique show examples of different halftoning effects produced by varying the frequency and dot shape (in step 5) and the intensity of the screen (in step 7).

1. Open a color image.

2. From the Image menu, choose Calculate and then Duplicate. Choose *New* for the Destination and its channel. Click OK. You'll use this duplicate image to create the black-and-white halftone, which you will then combine with the original file to create the color halftone.

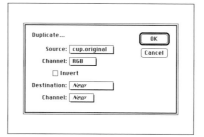

3. Convert the duplicated image to Gray Scale mode.

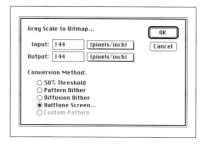

4. To create the halftone screen, select Bitmap from the Mode menu, and click the Halftone Screen option in the conversion dialog box. Leave the Input and Output values at their defaults (i.e., the current image resolution), and click OK.

Top: Variation 2 of this procedure, using a frequency of 30° lpi, an angle of 65°, and a Square dot shape.
Bottom (left to right): *1) Variation 2, using a frequency of 20 lpi, an angle of -45°, and the Line dot shape option. Magenta channel was duplicated instead of black. 2) Original procedure, using a frequency of 35 lpi, an angle of 20°, the Line dot shape option, and 15% of source 1 in step 7. 3) Variation 2, using the Cyan channel at a 40 lpi frequency, 45° angle, and the Line dot shape option.*

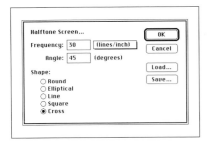

5. In the Halftone Screen dialog box, select the desired frequency, angle, and dot shape option (see the examples on the following pages). In this example, we used a frequency of 30 lines per inch, an angle of 45 degrees, and the Cross dot shape option. Click OK.

6. Convert the file back to Gray Scale mode using a Size Ratio of 1. This enables you to use the Calculate function in the next step to blend this halftone file with the original file. Save the file with the suffix *.halftone* for easy identification.

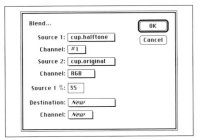

7. From the Image menu, choose Calculate and then Blend. Change Source 2 to the RGB channel of the original color file. (Source 1 is the halftone file; the Destination and its channel should be *New*.) Adjust the Source 1 % value to determine how much of the halftone will show through the image (we used 35%). Click OK.

8. If you don't like the results, close the new file without saving and repeat step 7 with a different Source 1 % value.

Variation 1: To halftone with a pattern, open a pattern file from the Photoshop Patterns folder. Small patterns are recommended. Select the pattern (⌘A), and choose Define Pattern from the Edit menu.

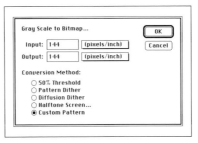

Follow steps 1-4 of this procedure using the Custom Pattern option when converting from Gray Scale to Bitmap mode in step 4.

Follow steps 6-8 to blend the images together.

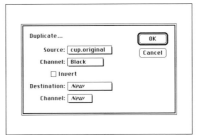

Variation 2: To create a halftone screen in a single color channel, start with a CMYK image. Duplicate the channel in which you want the halftone screen into a new file. In this example, we duplicated the black channel into a new file.

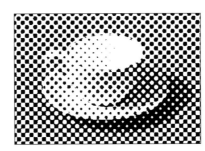

Convert the file to Bitmap mode using the Halftone Screen conversion option. Here, we used a frequency of 15 lines per inch and the Round dot shape option.

Convert the file back to Gray Scale mode; then duplicate it back into the original channel. Return to the CMYK channel (⌘0) to see the results.

The examples here were created using the halftoning procedure with different frequencies and dot shapes (in step 5) and different intensities of the halftone channel (in step 7). All examples were produced at an image resolution of 200 pixels per inch and using a 45-degree halftone screen angle. The frequency is indicated in lines per inch — a frequency of 40 or less is recommend to avoid moiré patterns in the printed artwork.

Original

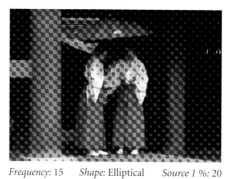
Frequency: 15   *Shape:* Elliptical   *Source 1 %:* 20

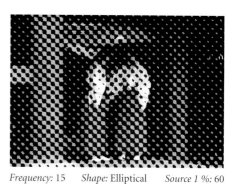
Frequency: 15   *Shape:* Elliptical   *Source 1 %:* 60

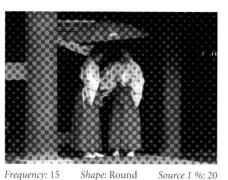
Frequency: 15   *Shape:* Round   *Source 1 %:* 20

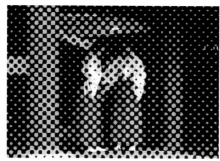
Frequency: 15   *Shape:* Round   *Source 1 %:* 60

Frequency: 25   *Shape:* Elliptical   *Source 1 %:* 20

Frequency: 25   *Shape:* Elliptical   *Source 1 %:* 60

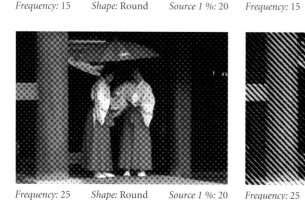
Frequency: 25   *Shape:* Round   *Source 1 %:* 20

Frequency: 25   *Shape:* Round   *Source 1 %:* 60

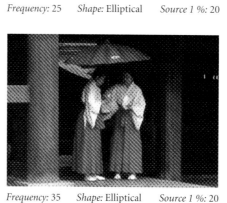
Frequency: 35   *Shape:* Elliptical   *Source 1 %:* 20

Frequency: 35   *Shape:* Elliptical   *Source 1 %:* 60

Frequency: 35   *Shape:* Round   *Source 1 %:* 20

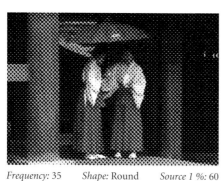
Frequency: 35   *Shape:* Round   *Source 1 %:* 60

Frequency: 15   *Shape:* Line   *Source 1 %:* 20

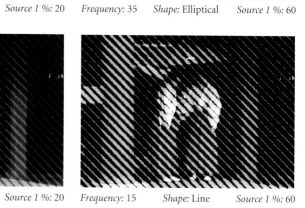
Frequency: 15   *Shape:* Line   *Source 1 %:* 60

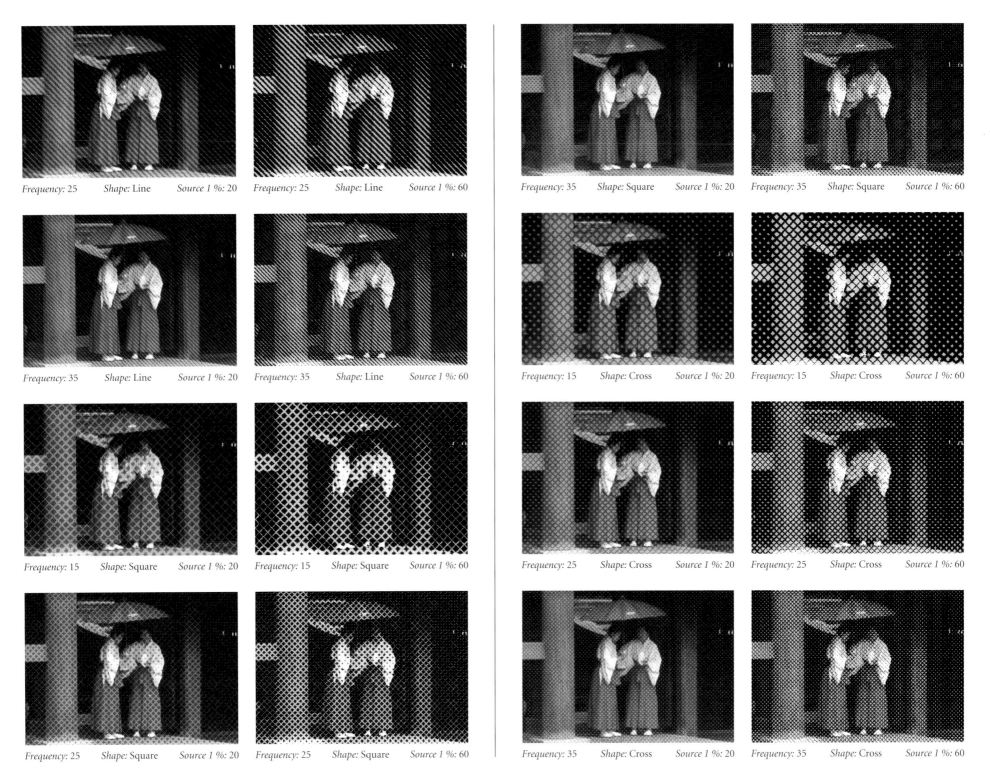

Frequency: 25   *Shape:* Line   *Source 1 %:* 20

Frequency: 25   *Shape:* Line   *Source 1 %:* 60

Frequency: 35   *Shape:* Square   *Source 1 %:* 20

Frequency: 35   *Shape:* Square   *Source 1 %:* 60

Frequency: 35   *Shape:* Line   *Source 1 %:* 20

Frequency: 35   *Shape:* Line   *Source 1 %:* 60

Frequency: 15   *Shape:* Cross   *Source 1 %:* 20

Frequency: 15   *Shape:* Cross   *Source 1 %:* 60

Frequency: 15   *Shape:* Square   *Source 1 %:* 20

Frequency: 15   *Shape:* Square   *Source 1 %:* 60

Frequency: 25   *Shape:* Cross   *Source 1 %:* 20

Frequency: 25   *Shape:* Cross   *Source 1 %:* 60

Frequency: 25   *Shape:* Square   *Source 1 %:* 20

Frequency: 25   *Shape:* Square   *Source 1 %:* 60

Frequency: 35   *Shape:* Cross   *Source 1 %:* 20

Frequency: 35   *Shape:* Cross   *Source 1 %:* 60

Color trapping and overprinting

Software needed: Adobe Illustrator 3.2, Adobe Separator 3.0.4

STROKE WEIGHT	TRAP IN INCHES	TRAP IN POINTS	SHAPES	LINES	TYPE
.4	.003	.2			a
.6	.004	.3			a
.8	.005	.4			a
1.0	.007	.5			a
1.5	.01	.75			a
2.0	.014	1.0			a
3.0	.021	1.5			a

When examining printed artwork, you'll often notice registration problems in areas where two colors meet. These problems are usually caused by the paper stretching or shifting slightly on the printing press. Traditionally, the color prepress operator has compensated for potential registration problems in the printed artwork by under- and overexposing certain areas of the film to create "trap" or "spread."

With color separation capabilities now included with many graphics programs, designers and production artists often have the option of creating trap themselves before printing film. Whether you are creating trap in Adobe Photoshop or Adobe Illustrator, it's important to work closely with the printer who will be printing the final artwork. The printer can help you locate areas in the artwork that need trap and determine how much trap they need. In addition, the printer can tell you what CMYK percentages to use to create a four-color black.

This section provides guidelines for creating trap in Adobe Illustrator. If you are unfamiliar with the basics of creating trap in Illustrator, see chapter 2 of the Adobe Illustrator Color Guide before reading this section. We also recommend showing the chart on this page to your printer so that you can figure out together what stroke weight will give the best results.

Finally, make sure that you know how the version of Adobe Separator you are using overprints black. Macintosh versions of Separator created before version 3.0.4 overprint black by default, while later versions (including all Windows versions) do not. Check the version number you are using, and see the color guide or the addendum that came with your program for information on what the default is and how to override it.

How a stroked path will print

It's important to remember that the stroke "straddles" the path – that is, when using stroked paths to create trap, half the line weight is inside the path, and the other half is outside the path. You therefore need to specify a stroke weight that is twice the amount of trap you want. For example, if you need .5-point spread trap, paint your shape with a 1-point stroke that overprints.

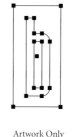

Artwork Only

Diagrammed preview

Stroke width
Path
Trap

Printed piece

Using four-color blacks

If you are printing process colors, you can avoid some registration problems by using a black that contains percentages of cyan, magenta, and yellow with 100% black. In general, misregistration is less noticeable if there is at least one shared color between adjacent shapes. The four-color black is also a much richer black than 100% black alone.

100% Black

30% Cyan
100% Black

20% Cyan
15% Magenta
15% Yellow
100% Black

Butt fit

Use this type of trap when your printer provides trap electronically or photomechanically.

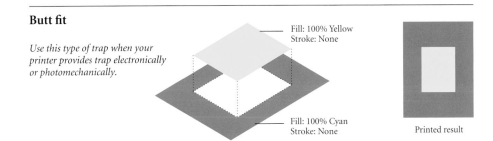

Fill: 100% Yellow
Stroke: None

Fill: 100% Cyan
Stroke: None

Printed result

Spread

Use when the background is darker than the object on top of it.

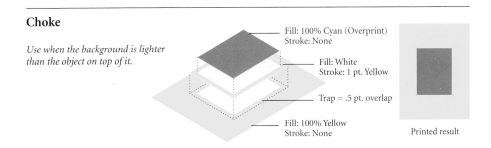

Fill: 100% Yellow
Stroke: 1 pt. Yellow
(Overprint)

Trap = .5 pt. overlap

Fill: 100% Cyan
Stroke: None

Printed result

Choke

Use when the background is lighter than the object on top of it.

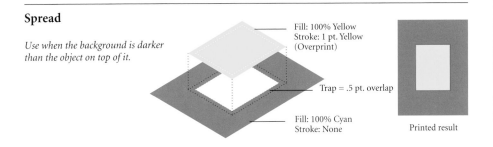

Fill: 100% Cyan (Overprint)
Stroke: None

Fill: White
Stroke: 1 pt. Yellow

Trap = .5 pt. overlap

Fill: 100% Yellow
Stroke: None

Printed result

Black lines overprint
(color background)

Use when the design contains many different color tints and the illustration style allows.

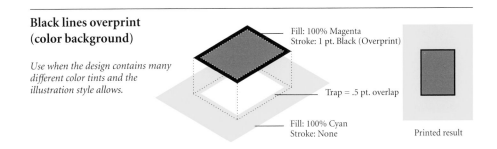

Fill: 100% Magenta
Stroke: 1 pt. Black (Overprint)

Trap = .5 pt. overlap

Fill: 100% Cyan
Stroke: None

Printed result

Black lines overprint
(four-color black background)

Use when your illustration or type is reversed out of a four-color black background.

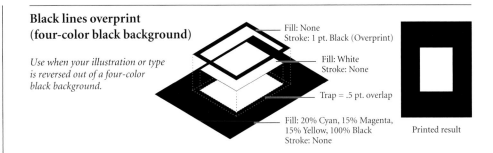

Fill: None
Stroke: 1 pt. Black (Overprint)

Fill: White
Stroke: None

Trap = .5 pt. overlap

Fill: 20% Cyan, 15% Magenta,
15% Yellow, 100% Black
Stroke: None

Printed result

Overprinting with
shared colors

When overprinting process color mixes that share common ink colors, the percentage of the topmost layer's shared color prints where the shared colors overlap — that is, the overprint feature does not affect common colors that overlap.

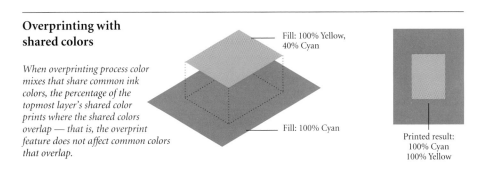

Fill: 100% Yellow,
40% Cyan

Fill: 100% Cyan

Printed result:
100% Cyan
100% Yellow

Overprinting with
uncommon colors

When overprinting process color mixes or custom colors that do not share common inks colors, the overprint color is added to the background color.

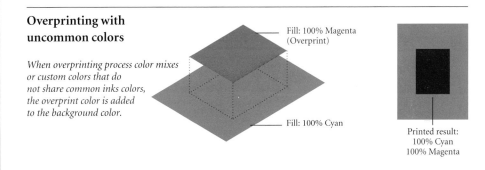

Fill: 100% Magenta
(Overprint)

Fill: 100% Cyan

Printed result:
100% Cyan
100% Magenta

Trapping lines

Use when printing lines on a colored or black background.

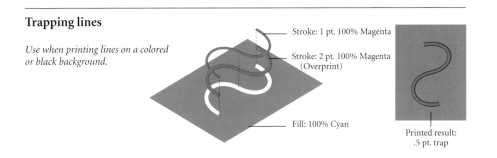

Stroke: 1 pt. 100% Magenta

Stroke: 2 pt. 100% Magenta
(Overprint)

Fill: 100% Cyan

Printed result:
.5 pt. trap

Index

Colophon

This book was designed and produced using Adobe Illustrator, Adobe Photoshop, Adobe Type Manager, and FrameMaker® on a Macintosh IIci. The Adobe Original typefaces Minion™ and Minion Expert are used throughout the book.

Final film was printed at 150 lines per inch on a Scitex RIP by FilmCraft, San Jose, California. Final film for the duotone, tritone, and quadtone section was printed at 175 lines per inch on an Agfa® SelectSet 5000 using Adobe Accurate Screens™ technology.

The book was printed by Shepard Poorman, Indianapolis, Indiana.